"Emotionally charged yet bu[...]
Flawed Perfection is beautif[...]
relative to anyone navigating the journey from trauma to triumph. Sound the alarm! Angel Runnels has boldly and honestly, without fear, found her authentic self. She no longer dwells in the expectations of others or societal norms and has overcome the self-loathing triggered by familiar faces. She is free."

—Madge Atkinson
Co-founder and senior pastor of Unlimited Ministries

"Wow! What an amazing young woman, with such a fighting spirit. The way she has been able to move forward in life is amazing. Such a testament to her strength and character. Angel does not shy away from just telling it like it was. She's open about what was done to her, how it happened, what she felt. When fear comes knocking on the door, let faith handle it."

—Bob Sawyer
Managing director of Trinity Investments,
former chairman of Mississippi Public Broadcasting

"Angel has exposed herself to herself and the world, without fear of what or whom. She writes with courage, knowing she isn't only writing for her healing, but for us all."

—Makalani
Abstract artist-creator of Visual Love Art

"Anyone who has gone through trauma within the 'safety spaces' of their family can relate to Angel's experiences. And those that know someone who has, can have a better understanding of how they feel, live, and cope. *Flawed Perfection* is written with raw unfiltered emotions. Grab the tissues, buckle up, and get ready to let go."

—Maureen C.

"Ms. Runnels beautifully writes of her soul-searching journey into life trauma. Uncommon honesty and unwavering courage carry her through the journey. This is a gritty labor of love that shows her humanity rise from the emotional wreckage in her wake."

—Dr. Patrick Evans

"Angel takes you on a journey through the confined spaces of expression. *Flawed Perfection* is raw and relatable and shows that although life can be messy, you can remain a badass."

—k.h.

"Angel's honesty took my breath away—page after page. It's not often we hear such brutal, raw, tender truth. She made me laugh, cry, think, hope, and dream new dreams for myself. This book, and Angel's life, is a beautiful testimony to the human spirit and its power to rise up and heal."

—Meredith D.

"*Flawed Perfection* is humanity in all its violent, triumphant, and inspiring savagery. Runnels bares her scars for the world. In doing so, the author provides a road map for those who have also stared into the gaping mouth of hell and walked away. Her journey teaches her, and those who follow it, that survival is one thing, living is another. There is beauty in our scars."

—Stuart Reb Donald

Chef, author, and host of Sip & Chew with Mike and Stu

"Angel boldly and bravely shares her journey in a no-holds-barred, soul-baring style. Written with a voice that is uniquely her own, she manages to capture both the raw ugliness of trauma and the resilient hopefulness of growth. Her memoir is a compelling must-read, and any reader with their fair share of baggage will find her story instantly and undeniably relevant and relatable."

—Krystal S.

Flawed Perfection

Flawed Perfection

LOVE HEALS ALL WOUNDS

Angel Runnels

Consulting by Freedom Press.

Editing by Steph Spector.

Cover Art by Makalani.

Author Photo by Laura DeMerchant

Cover and interior design by Charissa Newell, twolineSTUDIO.

Printed in the United States of America.

Ebook: 978-1-7375963-0-1
Paperback: 978-1-7375963-1-8
Hardback: 978-1-7375963-2-5
Audiobook: 978-1-7375963-3-2

Dedication

Flawed Perfection is dedicated to those of us who did not give up. It is dedicated to those of us who build other women up, who keep going after their dreams, who keep pursuing their own version of happiness each day. Little by little, one by one, we build a better tomorrow for ourselves, and for all of those who will come after. Yes! This jumping-off point is dedicated to us.

Cheers!

Table of Contents

Prologue

This story will be rough and raw, ugly tears and soft tears—until finally, bathed in the release and relief of telling the whole story, I satiate that deep longing for the gentle surrender that has escaped me for half a century. There will be no cascade of Mississippi dirt coming to hide this or sweep this shit under the rug. The vomit of my childhood will spew out and cover every inch of my adulthood, even after I "clean it up." I imagine that when we truly release, in truly owning our stories, our lives, our trauma—trauma that wasn't our own goddamn fault—life gets easier. It feels free. I'm talking about generational trauma, where only adults who never fixed their own traumas feed the mouths of their children like a momma bird feeding chicks the juicy worm. This worm should've been laced with tequila. At least then it might have been palatable.

Fighting to be human over and over again wears on your soul. Sooner or later, those crossroads begin to blend, get blurrier, and it's harder to discern the good way or the dark way. Maybe the spewing of my truth, the freeing of that truth like a bird that's been locked in the cage of my soul, will lead another desperately lost and wounded soul to some much needed light. To the soft, warm, sweet, secure light of being a human again. A human unafraid to love, or trust, or cry, or laugh, or fly like a banshee through the never-ending skies, singing that Tom Petty song about how I "won't back down."

It is time for the wild banshee, for the hot tears, for the all-consuming love and the blissful joy, for the pure freedom of release from these demons that have haunted me for lifetimes. Focusing on the "good" is what has kept me human all of these decades. I chose to pay more attention to the things that felt good. Had I not, the six-blanket-deep darkness would have swallowed me whole, sinking into the depths from which there would be no coming back.

My fervent hope is that all of us who have endured the deep oceans of trauma are able to swim out beyond the islands of regret and shame, shedding our armor before we leave this lifetime behind us. With this book, it is my attempt to release myself from my generational trauma, provide an open door for others to walk through and release their trauma, so that we all may shed our armor and live an amazing life without regrets. If only, is my wish . . .

Introduction

Back then, it was considered just another backwards, podunk town in south Mississippi. Rumor was that back in the fifties, there were already casinos there, and the military was the only thing that kept that place alive. If that's what you call "alive." Not sure what happened between then and when I showed up in the late sixties, but the casinos were long gone. The whole town revolved around the first and the fifteenth of the month since that was when the military got paid. Maybe we noticed those twice monthly revolutions because our families weren't part of the already affluent crowd. Not even close. We were second-rate citizens even within our own clans, especially if you were a female. Being a female meant they told you when and how your life was going to be; too bad if you didn't like it. You should have been born a man, or you better start acting like one—one with solid brass balls the size of Texas.

I wish I could tell you this story took place a long, long time ago, but that's not the truth. This story is based on the last half of the twentieth century, for fuck's sake! How could we have let this happen this way? I guess it's Mississippi, or the Deep South in general. Generations of trauma lie in this toxic soil. Its secrets are deep, dark, and rich. It's been turned and toiled year after year, expecting a better crop to grow each time, hoping for some good, rich bottom soil to begin to hide the secrets. Or maybe, it's time to expose those secrets.

That time has definitely come.

The time has come to heal the soil. It must be given proper nutrients, turned under every season, allowed to rest, tended to with proper crop rotation, sun, and water. And then it will yield the most fertile, rich, black gold. Black gold, where anything you burden it with will grow and flourish without hesitation, much like a woman. Anything you give her will be nurtured into something a thousand times more beautiful than ever imagined. Especially a woman who has done the necessary work to heal her past, heal her shadow, and walk with grace in spite of the crippling shame, the endless guilt, the abuse, and neglect; bruised and damaged, she still holds her head high as the tears stream from her golden eyes shining from the depths of the truth only her soul knows.

The Soul Knows

♥

My earliest memory was from around age two. Apparently, we aren't supposed to remember anything before about five or six—but I remember it all. I had gotten a cut earlier that day out in the fields behind the house. We had a few rabbits in cages back there and some horses, too. Mostly overgrown crabgrass and dandelion weeds, although the weeds were my favorite—that's what you make secret wishes on!

When I came back inside, Mom put some mercurochrome on my cut. It wasn't a bad cut, and that stuff stung like nothing else even though it wasn't "supposed to sting." She was always caring enough to blow her cool breath on it, though. Not sure that actually helped, but the nurturing gesture made me feel better nonetheless.

When she was done, she set the bottle of Not Supposed to Sting on top of our old console record player. You know, the kind with the lift-up tops on each end and the sliding front doors covered with latticework and velvet, fake wood all around to make it look extra fancy.

Later that night, I climbed onto the top of that console record player and sat up there, working on the lid for that stinging bullshit medicine she'd used on me just hours earlier. I poured that shit out! I poured that shit out all over the dark blue drapes with the brown-stained white sheers underneath. I remember my mom coming into the room and sneaking up on me. It made me jump when I heard her voice, but I sat there, holding that bottle and staring at her, not able to physically move.

That was the first time my soul left my body and watched from across the room. It wasn't that she did anything other than scold me and take the bottle away with whatever was left of that nasty shit. It's just that some part of me knew, for the first time, that I should get used to being outside of myself if I wanted to survive this life.

That old white house sat way off the road and had a drive-through carport that led to the backyard. There was an old dirt road off to one side that led to only god knows where. On the other side, a good three hundred yards or so away, lived my great-grandparents. The old house had big beautiful windows facing the front yard. I remember a few times my dad coming home, raising hell and being really loud, and I remember my mom being pregnant.

I remember our rabbits dying in those cages, coming out to find them just dried and crusty there on the bottom wires with their skin molding itself around the scorching metal. My guess is they died from the Miss'ippi heat. Even with enough water and food, there was never enough shade or airflow in that godforsaken place.

I don't remember too much else about that house except when I was older. Whenever we heard that old Dave Frizzell song about hiring a wino to decorate our home, that was always the house I imagined he was singing about.

We moved around a lot when I was really young. I'm not sure why. We just seemed to be in a new place a lot. Maybe that's why I've never really fully settled anywhere as an adult?

The next place I remember was an old, brown shake shingle house. It sat right in the corner at the fork in the road, smothered by the tallest, always-swaying pine trees. I just knew one of those was going to swing down and snatch me out of my bed one day. They were alive and they were wild, and I could feel it.

That house must've been far enough away from my grandparents because I remember my aunts and uncles coming over more at that house—long, loud nights of playing cards. I always got to stay up with the adults. That's what the oldest kids do, right? I also remember an old bean bag chair. That was *my spot*.

Sometimes one of the adults would come over and read to me or have me try and read to them. I think it was their way of trying to get me to go to sleep. There was no way I was going to sleep and miss out on any of that activity! They were laughing, talking and having fun . . . and there weren't too many of those times, so I chose to enjoy them when they came. Probably the first and the last time I ever just "went with the flow."

I must have been getting close to four or five because they kept asking if I was in kindergarten yet. I would say no. When I asked my parents why I wasn't in kindergarten, my dad replied, "You were too smart for kindergarten. They said you'd have to wait until first grade." Back then, kindergarten wasn't a requirement, and my birthday fell at such a time that I would have been a year behind those of my age group if I had waited until I was old enough to attend kindergarten. First grade wasn't so strict on the age requirement then, either.

I didn't know he was lying to me about why I didn't go to kindergarten. Nonetheless, I was filled with a false sense of pride and invincibility. I could handle anything—my dad said I was smart!

After that, we moved into the white house diagonally from Grandma and Grandpa in D'Lo, Mississippi. By this time, my sister and brother were both in this world with me. Most weekends, I would help my sister out of her crib, and sometimes we would go get our brother too, but we would walk down the gravel road to Grandma's for fresh scratch biscuits and gravy. Sometimes, it was syrup, butter, and biscuits. The best smells always came from Grandma's house, and almost always the best food! Biscuits, beans, and greens; although the greens had a very distinct smell that most don't care for even today. Biscuits, Beans, & Greens sounds like a good Southern cookbook just waiting to happen.

They also let us drink coffee! Grandma liked her coffee straight black, nothing yummy in there. Grandpa? He drank his sugar with a little coffee. We hung out there until our parents came over to get us. We weren't hard to find; wherever food and Grandma were, we were bound to be there, too. Easier times back then. No one ever worried about someone stealing us kids off the street. This same family would also tell us to go play in the street because anyone who took us would surely bring us back quickly. I absorbed this into my invincibility cloak, too . . . no one could ever harm me, and also, no one would ever want me.

It was in this house that I realized I never wanted children of my own. While the adults gathered for the holidays, myself being the oldest grandchild, I became the dedicated babysitter. My mother was the oldest of six children, two of whom had five children each. I was changing diapers and making milk bottles before I was even eight years old. Snotty noses, nasty diapers, all the crying, all the screaming . . . and they never listened to me when I gave them orders. For fuck's sake! Wasn't it beaten into them that they obey their elders, like it was beat into me?

One night, we were telling ghost stories on the screened-in front porch. If we had been up north somewhere, we would have all been cuddled under warm heavy blankets. We weren't. We were in south-central Mississippi, where even the devil won't visit. Not because it's considered the "Bible Belt," but because it's too fucking hot for at least eleven and a half months of every fucking year.

It was a big, grand front porch with a massive Spanish oak out front with giant arms reaching over the porch, providing welcomed shade and sometimes even a gentle breeze. I think it was Thanksgiving that year. The adults were all inside at the kitchen table playing cards, drinking, talking, and laughing loud enough for us to hear them clear out on the front porch. In an effort to keep the other kids entertained and contained, I suggested we tell ghost stories. After all, the adults had already scolded me more than once for not keeping all of us kids outside on the porch. Ghost stories seemed like a good choice since you weren't allowed to be a pussy in this family. Oddly, I never felt that to be a negative—do they realize that's where babies come from? Maybe that added to my invincibility cloak, too?

The wind was howling that night. In the faraway distance, there were dogs howling, too. All of us were gathered on blankets out on the front porch. We sat very close together, scooched right next to each other. After all, we were telling ghost stories.

The wind kept that majestic Spanish oak whistling its leaves in a soft, gentle lullaby just enough for Southern ears to hear. One of the uncles had told me a ghost story earlier that day, and as I began to retell the story, the younger ones scooched even closer to me. The story was something about a man who died because the murderer cut off his arm; his arm was made of gold, which is why the greedy murderer cut it off in the first place. At least, that's all I could think about when they told the story to me.

These children didn't care why the arm had been cut, just that someone had lost their arm and now the dead guy was looking for his lost limb. As the intensity of the story grew, all ten of the younger children leaned in closer to me, and me toward them. Just then, that old Spanish oak let loose one of her massive branches, and it crashed onto the parched ground with a giant thud that shook the whole porch.

All at once, all of us ran screaming into the house toward the adults. Thankfully, I didn't get into trouble for that one. Not even for the ghost story. When we all became teenagers, we laughed about that night—still burned into our memories, like the hot poker from an out-of-control fire blazing across the landscape of our childhood in podunk Mississippi.

And So It Begins

♥

*A*round age six, my parents moved us to the Gulf Coast of Mississippi. My mom made our clothes and dressed my sister and me as twins even though there are nearly two full years between us. I hated that. Even way back then, it seemed as if she was trying to bring me down to my sister's level, knowing all along we would never be anything close to the same. She was not my twin then, and she definitely isn't now. My sister and I have always been night-and-day different—we always will be.

We bought our first house just before my seventh birthday in a middle-class neighborhood with lovely brick homes everywhere and perfect, tree-lined streets. Most importantly, this new house was walking distance from the elementary school. Dad liked the house because it also had an inground pool. Not just any inground pool, either; this one was a full twelve feet deep on one end and up to four feet on the other by the steps. There were woods behind the six-foot privacy fence that led to the road we called "the curves." Otherwise, this house was just like all the others: three bedrooms, one bath, and a carport that some residents had turned into a full garage, although we never did that.

That year, I was allowed to have a birthday party with my new friends from school and the neighbor kids. I don't remember much about that birthday, just that I received a pretty jewelry box with a dancing ballerina, and I got seven dollars. In CASH! Now we're getting somewhere.

Within a week of that birthday, our house was robbed. On this particular evening, dad "worked late," and Mom was home with us kids. Dad working late just meant he was most likely out with one of his girlfriends. Mom and us three kids decided on pizza for dinner. This was way back before pizza delivery was even a thing, and there wasn't any call ahead, either. You had to drive there, order your pizza, and wait for it to be made. Can't even imagine that now.

We loaded into the car. I don't remember what the car was so much as I remember all three of us sitting in the backseat. We were all super tiny, so we fit easily, although that didn't prohibit the "stop touching me" game.

As we drove to the local Pizza Hut, we all sang along with Mom when the radio played "Delta Dawn." You know the one: *Delta Dawn, what's that flower you have on, could it be a faded rose from days gone by?* Those were fun times, when the rest of the world didn't seem to exist. It was only us and we were having fun. My brother, with his usual antics, made us all bust out in laughter as he made up new words to the song just as we pulled up into the parking lot.

Mom went in to order. The three of us stayed in the car. Just before she came back, I told my brother and sister that someone had just broken into the house. I'm not even sure where it came from; it just flew out of my mouth with wings created on its departure. Mom sat back down in the front seat. You could feel the energy thick now with fear. She asked what was going on, and I repeated myself.

"No," she said, brushing it off. "It's probably just that your dad is home now."

We sat in silence mostly after that, unable to recover from the fear energy. We were all too familiar with that energy, and the possibility of the violation taking place in our new home was harder to bear as our hopes for a new beginning were being drained from our young souls right there in the Pizza Hut parking lot.

Our drive home was not quiet. I could no longer hold in the visions flashing through my head. It was as if I were seeing our new home through the eyes of one of the robbers. It was so real and so vivid, crystal clear to me.

I began telling them where the robbers were in our house and that there were three of them in total. I could see the van behind the privacy fence, but I didn't recognize the van or the men. I knew they were all tall men, though. Of course, everyone would have been giants to a tiny seven-year-old like me.

I could see as they walked through the house, and I could hear them discussing what each of them was going to take from the house. I allowed those visions to flow from my tiny, seven-year-old lips with the certainty of an old woman who had already seen and done some shit and knew what the fuck she was talking about. I was *that* certain that what I was seeing and speaking was the absolute truth of what was happening. I watched as these men walked into my bedroom and picked up my new, fancy jewelry box and took my seven dollars, throwing the beautiful ballerina onto the floor, still dancing.

How could she dance at a time like this?

I watched as they went into my parent's bedroom closet and began passing out the rifles, shotguns, and pistols that were kept there. They loaded the bow and arrows and rifled through some of the drawers. As I described all of these details, my brother and sister began to cry. I saw them unplugging the television just as my mom told me to stop talking. She said none of that was happening, and it was just the new place, and we just hadn't had time to settle in there yet. As we rounded the curves, all of the lights were on in the backyard overlooking the twelve-foot deep swimming pool. Mom tried to reassure us three by saying our dad must be home now and was cleaning the pool, but I knew it wasn't true.

As we pulled into the driveway, dad's car was not there. My brother and sister began to cry harder now. I knew they could feel what I had been saying was the truth, but now it was undeniable. Mom pulled all the way under the carport and ordered us to stay in the car. We all began to cry then. Why would she go in there? They have our guns! She could be killed and leave us alone with that horrible excuse of a human being for our only parent! What the fuck is she thinking?

STOP! MOM! STOP! DON'T GO IN THERE!

We all cried louder, but she didn't listen.

We weren't afraid for our own lives. Only hers. A few seconds later, our dad pulled up. It was one of the few times we'd actually be glad to see him.

This was the first time my psychic abilities showed themselves. I was afraid but also not afraid. It seemed to be so much a part of me, so clear, so vivid, so very, very real. No one ever spoke about what I had said that night, and to my knowledge, our mom never told our dad either.

The night of the robbery, after the cops came, reports were taken and all had gone; our neighbors were out in their yards watching the spectacle that had just unfolded with the new people. Our bully of a father needed someone to blame, someone to take his frustration out on. With everyone watching, it couldn't be our mom or us kids this time. He decided it was going to be the neighbor across the street, a little man, meek and mild. My dad stood in the yard yelling at him, saying he knew he was in on this and that he would find out and he would kill him and his friends too. Yelling, he told him he wanted his stuff back and would be coming after him and his family if our stuff wasn't returned. It was mortifying. There we were, standing in the front yard of our new home, in our new neighborhood, with our new neighbors all watching, and he was setting the scene forever for the non-drunk, yet somehow still belligerent asshole who had just moved in.

Nope. There was no getting out of this white-trash moment with any pride or dignity. A seven-year-old, who just had a party for her birthday, with all the kids in the neighborhood and at school . . . this moment would never be forgotten. This was a time when I was wishing I had been adopted. At least then, it wouldn't be completely my fault. Dissociation would have been accepted since he wasn't "blood kin." But unfortunately, I wasn't adopted. In fact, I was and am the spitting image of my mother. Which, in hindsight, probably fueled his rage toward me over the years.

The next few years in the beige brick house seemed to settle down a bit except for the fighting between my parents. They also decided to add a second story to the house. In hindsight, maybe it never settled down at all; it could explain my need as an adult to always be moving. Progress, right? The construction was slow, and we had several contractors because my dad always fought with them over something. The fighting between our parents was always brutal, to the degree that dad would wake us up—on a school night—and make us stand in the kitchen to watch as he beat our mother bloody.

He even went so far one night as to make us watch, telling us she had "fought back" that night, so he was going to teach her a lesson by putting her head on a plate. He wanted us to watch to make sure we knew what he was capable of. Thankfully, he didn't cut her head off. It was "only" two black eyes and a busted lip. Probably some bruised ribs too. But she would never complain, lest he set in on her again.

As children, we were all filled with fiery rage and red-hot anger and had no idea how to get it out in a healthy way. Generations of abuse, anger, rage, and fear fed into our whole bodies. Blood, bones, hair, teeth—every organ absorbed the hate and dysfunction of our surroundings. We were trapped and unable to tell any other adults what was going on for fear of . . . well, the night Uncle Tommy came over made it very clear what would happen if we told. So we took it out on each other and on ourselves.

That one night during a particularly bad fight, we called my dad's brother, Uncle Tommy, while a fight was happening, thinking he would come help. We were scared. Uncle Tommy came over, but instead of helping Mom, he held her down while dad continued to punch her, giving her a couple of black eyes. A couple of black eyes, turning into my dad's signature move for beating a helpless woman, in case we needed to know what a "real man" could do to a strong woman. He told us to wait outside, but we, of course, watched every blow through the window. We were three young children in our pajamas, just waiting for it all to be over, hoping that our mother would still be alive when it was.

On another night, Mom called the local police. They came, seeing the black eyes, all of the blood, and the scared children. Yet somehow, dad was a smooth talker, and we were all too afraid to speak up. The cops left without doing anything about any of it. It probably didn't help that our parents were the accountants for the local police force. The cops left, and she got a few more back-handed smacks just for being a snitch. #snitchesgetmorestitches

It would be better if I could tell you he was a raging alcoholic, or maybe that he took copious amounts of drugs, but this was just the tip of the iceberg when it came to his cruelty-filled rages toward our mother and us children. This was what happened if we questioned his authority. But somehow, instinctively, I always knew to question authority.

Drowning Out The Innocence

♥

Throughout those years in the beige brick house with the big pool in the backyard, we had numerous babysitters. Babysitters came and went—mostly went because of dad's advances on them. One even left before our parents made it home. She was courteous enough to call our mom first to tell her she was leaving. The babysitter told us to tell our mom that she loved her boyfriend too much to continue working for our parents. Another babysitter knew she wouldn't get paid if she didn't have sex with him, so she took a knife and cut open our piggy banks. She took every last cent and hid the slashed-open, pink and blue pig-shaped banks behind a hydrangea bush in the corner of the backyard. Several others just never showed back up.

One summer afternoon, when the babysitter just never showed up, our dad came home from work early. My brother, sister, and I were swimming in the pool. I was about to turn ten. We didn't need a babysitter anyway, did we?

We were screaming, laughing, splashing, and having a great afternoon. Our dad came to the screen door looking out onto the pool with an angry look on his face. We weren't sure what we had done wrong. Maybe nothing—but it was always hard to know for sure. He angrily told me to get out of the pool and come inside. I had a sick feeling in my stomach, thinking I was about to get one of those beatings he gave our mom. I did as I was told while my brother and sister stayed motionless in the pool, with panicked looks on their tiny little faces.

Sensing their trepidation, he told them to stay outside and keep playing. He instructed them not to come inside. I was scared, shaking, and dripping wet from the pool, my feet leaving prints across the dark green, paisley kitchen carpet as he led me to the back bedroom. The kitchen carpet, already really ugly, was now wet with a shivering nine-year-old's footprints. Maybe I should have been worried about getting into trouble for getting the carpet wet, but we weren't really taught how to take care of things, especially not one another or ourselves.

He took me to our parents' bedroom in the back of the house and closed the door. Through the solar-screened window, I could still see and hear my brother and sister, now back to playing joyfully in the pool. At least they didn't have to endure this. He took off his pants—he never wore underwear—and then he laid on the bed. He laid on his side of the bed, the side closest to the door, and put his right arm across his forehead like he had done many times before. Then he told me to suck on his bare cock. I had no idea what he was asking me to do. He softened his voice and told me to hold it with one hand and put my mouth on it.

I was trying so hard not to vomit. *What is this?* I thought. *This is really gross.* He then told me to move my hand up and down and not to use my teeth. I did as I was told, still shivering from the cool air brushing across nine-year-old wet skin. I must not have been doing a very good job because he told me to stop. It seemed like an eternity. Then he told me not to tell anyone because if I did, we'd both get into trouble.

I had no doubt of the trouble I would be in with *him* if I told anyone. I was more worried about what he would do to my brother and sister if I told. He told me to go back outside and play and close the door on my way out. As I left that room, uncontrollable shivers ran through and over my tiny nine-year-old body. I really wanted to vomit now. I was too scared to focus on what had just happened and too scared that if I didn't get out of there right then, he would make me come back into that bedroom.

I ran outside to my brother and sister. They had no idea they were my safe place.

My skin was dry now, but I felt gross, like I needed a shower. The only bathroom was right outside his bedroom, though. There was no way I was going anywhere near there again. I lied to my brother and sister when they asked what he wanted. I don't even remember what I told them, but it definitely wasn't the truth. Guess this was my dad's way of forcing me to be a liar, like him. The depth of this psychological truth would haunt me for at least another decade.

I knew for sure that if I told anyone, I would probably end up buried in the backyard in front of my mother and my siblings, to make damn sure they didn't talk either. I could never look him in the eyes after that, not that it was easy before—but definitely not now. That was the only time that ever happened. I was in my forties before I ever told anyone about that day, and then, it was only under extreme duress. I like to think that it only happened the one time because he had a conscience somewhere underneath his own sordid layers of abuse and neglect. Who's to say for sure, though? I just don't have any good memories of him. And I prefer not to ever think of him—or that day—ever.

My mind raced every time I had to walk past their bedroom. It was as if it had demons inside, and we all knew it did. How could he even sleep in there knowing what he had done to me? I wondered if my mom would still sleep in there knowing what he had done.

Would she stay with him if I told? Or would he just kill us all and tell everyone we were murdered? Slaughtering us inside the house, leaving blood splatter on every wall, and then hiding our bodies, only to tell everyone how his wife stole his kids and ran off with some man she was cheating on him with?

Who was I kidding? I was never gonna tell. I was more worried about what he would do to my mom and my brother and sister if I told. But the stealing of his kids and running off was plausible. His usual M.O. was to project that shit onto my mom any chance he got. It was always she who was out running around on him, always she who was abusing him.

In late April of 1979, dad had a date planned. In his usual fashion, he beat Mom bloody and stormed out. We knew he would be gone for at least three days. Ironically, those were the most peaceful days—the ones without him there.

It was a big month for the Mississippi Gulf Coast. The 28th Annual Miss America pageant would be held at the Gulf Coast Coliseum that year. The whole town was on the pageant bandwagon. Dad's date was during this time.

When it came time to watch the pageant on television, Mom sat with us three kids. She only had one black eye this time, but it was still swollen and bruised. We were sitting on our old couch, watching the big screen in the quiet peace without our father. The big screen was one of those inverted televisions inside a box with a giant telescope thing coming out of it. The television was upside down in the box, and then the giant telescope reverted it upright and projected it onto a standing screen that was at least twenty times bigger than the television inside. It was a really cool thing. And a total eighties thing to have around.

I was too focused on survival to allow the luxury of learning or imagination to take place, or to learn or imagine how cool stuff worked. I had bigger things weighing on me, like survival. There was no room for learning or anything else to take place, nothing other than fear.

It was a school night, but Mom let us stay up late so we could all watch the pageant together. I think we even had popcorn that night. We watched the pageant, laughed, and talked all the way through.

Then the visions started again.

The sirens from the pageant started ringing through the streets about that same time. When the sirens started, I told Mom that dad had just been in a car accident. She didn't believe me and told me it was just the sirens for the pageant, and that his absence had me scared. But I knew I was right, and I started giving her details of the wreck. There were trees and other cars and a fancy car, and it looked like the big interstate and not the highway to Grandma's. The sirens were still blaring in the background, and I continued to describe our dad slumped over in a field or something. My brother and sister started crying. Mom told me to stop and made us all go to bed. After all, we had school tomorrow.

I couldn't sleep, though. I knew I was right. I wondered if he was dead. Maybe "hoped" is a better word. *Could this really be the end of our nightmare?* I thought. *Or maybe, if he survives, he would realize what a great family we could be and he'd be nicer to us and not hurt Mom so much.* Although we'd been to church with Grandma a few times and the Baptist neighbors a few times, too, we weren't much into praying in our household; after all, what was the use of prayer when the devil himself lived in your own home?

The next morning, Mobile Infirmary called to say that dad was there and in a coma. If he survived, he would be a paraplegic. It was May 1, 1979. I was about to turn ten, my sister was about to turn eight, and my brother six as of that April 17.

All I could think was *PULL THE FUCKING PLUG!*

But Mom had no intention of pulling that plug. Which only added to the suffering and trauma that my brother, sister, and I had to endure beyond this point. In hindsight, maybe she was hoping the same thing I was—that there was a sliver of hope he would come back as a better human.

The Bad Uncle

♥

*O*nce they *determined that* dad wasn't coming home anytime soon and Mom wasn't giving up on him, we were shipped to my grandparents. Thankfully—or not thankfully—we had a place to go other than the hospital with dad. Maybe not so thankfully, because it was summertime in middle Mississippi now. This place is a thousand degrees, and even hotter in the shade of the pecan trees. There was no such thing as a cooling breeze. Any breeze that did blow felt like you were standing next to the biggest bonfire the South ever had, with a fan blowing that stifling heat right onto your face. Like your face was melting, sliding off onto the hot, green grass squished between your steaming toes.

At Grandma's, my aunt and uncle lived just down the street. This aunt was the youngest of my mom's sisters. She was super skinny and very pretty, always loved kids, and was definitely one of the fun aunts. Her husband, though, was not a handsome man. He was tall with dark hair and crazy eyes. He was missing the end of one of his middle fingers. Not sure what happened there, and I didn't care, really.

When he would come around, he was very touchy-feely with all the women in a creepy way. Most adult women just stayed away from him. Oddly, no one bothered to protect us little girls from him. Maybe they thought we were safe since he had two daughters of his own? I don't think they were safe, either. He and my aunt had five children total: two girls, then three boys. He was always trying to make a fast buck doing odd jobs or selling this and that, but I don't think he ever kept a job for very long. I am pretty sure he swindled our all-too-trusting grandparents on more than one occasion, too.

I remember one time, Grandma had some old Confederate money in a box. She made the mistake of showing it to us at Christmas one year. The next day, he offered to take it and "have it appraised" for her. She let him take it. He brought back the fake stuff from Cracker Barrel. She never even questioned it. Many years later, when we pointed out to her that the money he brought back said "facsimile" on it, she said someone else must have stolen the old money.

He was the kind of swindler who made you feel like you needed a cold shower after you walked past him on the street. He oozed disgustingness.

He and my aunt had an old beat up VW van that was loud and sputtered a lot. Obviously, he wasn't a very good mechanic either. It was white or a light cream color. That summer, after we were sent to Grandma's because dear old dad was in a coma and our dutifully abused mother was unwaveringly by his side, that's when the predatory uncle took the opportunity to molest me. My aunt had gone to work that day. He did not—not sure he even had a job then, honestly. Grandma worked nights, so she was sleeping. All of us cousins were playing out in the yard.

The uncle drove up in the old van and asked if any of us wanted to learn how to drive. Of course we did! We all ran screaming toward the van. That's when he said it would be safer one at a time—you know, just in case we wrecked. He said he would start with the oldest. That would be me at the grown age of nearly ten. I remember I was wearing a pair of shorts and a little halter top with sandals. I hated sandals. I still do.

As I climbed into the van, he sat me between his legs in the driver's seat and hollered back to the other kids to stay out of the way. He told me to keep both hands on the steering wheel at all times, "so I didn't cause a wreck." He put one hand on my leg and pretended to hold the steering wheel. As we pulled away from the other kids, he moved his thumb under my little top and started playing with my nipples. He would move his hand around under my shirt, pretending he was doing nothing wrong. It felt completely wrong. It felt dirty and gross. But I was just a kid. What was I supposed to say or do? These aren't conversations I was taught to have, and there were no boundary lessons in my family, either. Even if there were, I am certain they would not have applied to us women.

After he made my tiny nipples hard, he slid his hand under my shorts and began fingering my vagina. That's when I started to squirm a bit and tried to move away. But I was "driving," and I was tucked tightly between his legs and pinned between him and the steering wheel, his legs tightening their grasp, holding me in place. I had no idea what was happening, but I didn't like it, and I said I wanted to go back. That's when he told me not to tell anyone, or we would both get into big trouble.

Fucker.

I doubted he even knew what "big trouble" was. He'd never seen my dad backhand my mom or heard him threaten us. What the fuck did he know about big trouble. In my little girl's mind, I was thinking maybe my dad could give him a good lashing for what he just did! I also knew my dad wasn't that kind of protective father; he was someone we needed protection from.

It was apparent that if you wanted protection in this family, you'd better learn to defend yourself—and fast!

Then, I began wondering if maybe the shame from the blow job was all over my face, and now every predator would be able to quickly find me, to see, or to somehow tell I was already soiled. Was the shame shining for all predators to see? If so, could the other victims see it, too? Or was there some sort of secret alliance the predators all subscribed to and were all part of? All women are fair game, and if they talk, they get stitches, extra beatings, and abuse—or death, leaving their daughters' (and sons') fates in the hands of those same terrible men.

At the end of the summer, I told my sister and one of my cousins, Paula. My sister got up before either Paula or I could and told the adults. I remember feeling relieved initially that someone knew, and that my secret was out. Then the adults started fighting out in the front yard. Screaming. Yelling. And I was the bad guy. I could hear my mom screaming that this happened to her, and "dammit, she didn't want it to happen to her children." I had no idea what she was talking about—she had never mentioned anything about any of that to us kids. She told my grandparents and the other adults that they were supposed to have protected us. My grandmother basically called me a liar and said my uncle would never do anything like that. It was then I realized being the favorite grandchild had its limits. My grandfather never said a word. It would be decades before I knew why.

Protective Oblivion

As the scorching hot Southern summer came to an end and it was time to go back to the coast and back to school, our dad had awakened from the coma, went into physical therapy, and began his recovery. Our mother dutifully by his side at every moment. I was struggling with my own emotions as my teenage years neared. I wished he'd died in that car wreck. *How much better off we could be without him!* I thought. Then came the suffocating guilt. I really struggled to just get out of bed every day. Protecting my brother and sister was the only reason I did. I was not even fucking eleven years old! I'd lived too much life already for my young heart and soul.

Once he was released from the hospital, dear old dad made sure to quickly squelch any hopes I had of him now being a better person. His anger had grown progressively more intense—as if that were even imaginable. He hated life and himself and all of us along with it.

One night, my mom left to go to the grocery store to buy milk for our breakfast the next day. He had been asleep in his chair. We didn't dare wake him. He woke up while she was gone and went into a rage about how long she had been gone and who she might've been with. He locked and bolted all of the doors and got his .30-06 rifle with full scope and sat on the small sofa in only his underwear and colostomy bag. He told the three of us that whoever let her in would be shot, too.

The three of us cried and waited, filled with anger, angst, and fear. My mind raced with images, like a chess game, of

what to do, when to do it, and how. After all, it was my job
to protect my brother and sister at all costs. I remember
wondering if I could get a job that would support the three
of us. Maybe then we would be okay? I mean, he was going
to jail after he killed our mom, so we would be orphans; the
thought of the pedo uncle taking us in sent chills all over me.
It provided me with even more resolve to just fucking do it
myself.

As Mom pulled up, my sister was the one who unlocked
the door and let her in, but all three of us were standing there.
He made Mom sit on the couch across from him and fired a
shot almost immediately. Thankfully, it was above her head . . .
a warning shot? Who knows, but his point was clear.

It was a school night. Mom made us all go to bed, as if we
could sleep wondering if we would wake up to only one parent
and the house splattered with bullets and blood.

The yelling that night was so intense we all ended up in
the same bed, crying for most of the night. School the next day
was so hard, but we didn't dare tell anyone what was going
on at home. That could result in death for one or all of us. On
top of that, after the accident, the pity from the whole fucking
town toward my dad was vomitous. They would never believe
he could do such a thing. I knew he would not hesitate to kill
us all, especially our mother. He might spare my little brother,
but only if he survived until the rest of us were dead. At the
young age of twelve, I believed that with all my heart.

As time passed, dad learned to walk with just the aid of a
cane and then completely on his own without the use of any
medical aids. The medical community declared him a "miracle"
with a strong will to live, which clearly fed his ego and resulted

in us being even more useless in his eyes. Although, as a bonus from the gods and because of his diagnosis, I was allowed to drive at fourteen years of age.

During my teenage isolation, I couldn't bring many friends home from school—not that I had that many, anyway. If I brought any female friends home, my dad would make passes at them. It was truly mortifying to me and caused me to isolate even more from the rest of the world. Loneliness was my only friend, and it was his fault.

As my little girl's body began to develop, to continue his torture of me, he would grab my tiny nipples, hard, and tell me those were *his* nipples. I remember wanting to slit his fucking throat during those times. Images flashed in my head of blood splattering across his La-Z-Boy recliner, those ugly green curtains, and those cigarette brown–stained white walls. A welcomed vision in those moments. Instead, I walked away with stinging tears in my eyes and filled with red-hot rage. My hands clenched into tiny little fists. My heart was broken that this man, who was supposed to love and protect me, was actually the one person who hated me the most. And the feeling was mutual.

Besides, I couldn't dare kill him now. He had garnered so much fucking sympathy from the community, and he presented well—at least in public. They would crucify me for "killing a cripple." No one had any idea what was going on behind those closed doors. Did anyone even care? He was a small-town hero now; my mom, brother, and sister, and I were just shit on his shingle and we were reminded of that fact every day.

My parents were self-employed before his accident; technically, now that he was disabled, he wasn't supposed to be working. It didn't really matter. My mom did all of the work before and after the accident. Now, my dad would just sit at his desk and play cards and say he was "disabled" and couldn't work anyway. He would say he was there for "security," although Mom was always at the other office across town. Who could blame her?

And besides, the only person she needed protection from was him.

My brother, being the youngest and the only boy, was obviously dad's favorite. My little sister—who carried baby dolls and preferred to stay inside and watch Mom cook, instead of be outside shooting guns and arrows—was picked on relentlessly by our dad. She had all of the protection Mom could offer, even though he had already proven that Mom could not stop him.

Being the oldest, I preferred to stay in the good graces of the abuser and learned quickly to master any challenge he gave me: guns, knives, bow and arrows, cussing, working on cars. Sadly, I wasn't learning so much as memorizing just enough to stay under the radar and out of his line of fire. Who could say if what he was teaching us was the actual truth anyway? Tough to imagine he had any idea what he was talking about, this useless excuse for a human being. With so little respect for him, I didn't dare take anything he said about real life as actual truth.

I began counting the days until I could escape this prison without going to a real prison. I had no idea how I was going to make it happen, or whether or not my brother and sister would be able to escape with me. It was clear Mom wasn't going to leave him, and the gods allowed him to live and come back to torture us more. That only left me to handle it myself. It made me hate the gods even more and question religion on a number of levels.

The chess game of how to kill him—quietly—and preferably without any evidence leading back to me or my mother, played out day after day in my head. Surely there was some type of poison I could slip in his sweet tea?

But what if my brother or sister accidentally drank it? Scratch that. What else could I do? Stabbing him in the eye with an ice pick was an option. Maybe I could offer to give him another blow job; that would get me close enough. He would be so distracted by the thought that I could easily sneak up on him with a blade or a pick. My rage toward him and also toward my mother filled every cell of my teenage body. Why wouldn't she leave him? Why did she feel it was okay for us to be treated this way, to live in this fear every day—waiting for him to get mad enough to kill us all?

That I was on heightened alert was an understatement.

The bit he taught me about working on cars seemed to come in handy for his continued abuse of our mother and his "date nights." Who would even *want* this cheating, lying, colostomy bag–wearing, need-a-shot-to-get-an-erection piece of shit, anyway? Who were these fucking women?

He taught me to pull the spark plugs out and remove the coil wire from the rotor cup. He taught me to do that when he wanted to go on a date and didn't want Mom to follow him. I was told to remove it and not tell anyone, which is exactly what I did.

One night, my dad left after a swift backhand for Mom. He hadn't told me to remove the plug, so I didn't. Mom loaded us kids up in the car, and we drove all over town looking for him. We found him at the library, and Mom parked right outside the window, where he sat with his latest girlfriend. The windows of the library were mirrored during the day, and since it was dark, we could see right through to the two of them at a table talking and holding hands. In hindsight, I think this was the beginning of the end for my mother.

I often wondered what wild stories he must be telling these women for them to be with him. Was it a tale of woe is me? One of heroism despite the odds against him?

So, after beating my wife in front of our children and going on a date with one of my girlfriends, I had a terrible car accident. Oh, yeah, and I made my oldest daughter give me a blow job on my way out the door. But don't worry about all of that nonsense. Let's go have fun. And let me tell you about how great I am because I recovered when they said I should be dead.

How do you spin *that* story?

What the actual fuck could he possibly have said that would make them want to be anywhere near him?

The First
And The Last
Beating

♥

With our everyday home life filled with rage, insecurity, and verbal and emotional abuse, we had no idea what to do when it started happening at school, too. This was especially true for my little brother.

After school one day, my brother came home really angry. He was being bullied at school by some bigger boys. We didn't know that at the time, and much like our home life, telling was not an option. #snitchesgetstitches

Learning all too well from our father, my brother knew it was time to physically abuse someone close by—preferably a woman—and my little sister was his usual target. He would pick a fight with my little sister, then call our dad for backup. Dad would get on the phone and tell me to "handle it." After his chat with dear old dad, my brother felt validated and continued his attack on my sister. I told her to go lock herself in the bathroom, sit on the floor, and put her feet on the toilet as a brace and her back against the door. Once she was safely inside the bathroom, my brother and I got into our first real fistfight with each other. I was fifteen, and he was ten.

In the most recent years, my dad would force my brother and me to practice football so my brother could be a better player. With my brother in full football gear (pads, helmet, mouthpiece) and me not covered or padded in any way, we would have to practice for hours with me taking a beating and trying not to hurt my little brother in the process. In hindsight, I suppose it helped my body process the rage I carried so deeply inside. It also made it extra clear how little my dad cared about me or my well-being on any level.

My little brother was very strong, and he was very angry that day after school. I also had a mouth full of braces—the old, metal, hard kind. As the punches flew, my sister screamed from the bathroom for us not to hurt each other. I guess our whole family had seen enough beatings.

Just then, my brother landed a punch right on my mouth, and I started bleeding from the cuts the braces made in my skin. When I saw the blood, I lost my temper and grabbed him, pinned him down, and started wailing on him. When I saw blood, I stopped. He immediately called our dad.

Dad rushed home. He ordered me into the kitchen along with my brother and sister. Both my brother and I had blood on our faces. It wasn't nearly as much blood as Mom always had on her face, but nonetheless, there was blood. I knew it was the beginning of something horrible. Dad pinned me into his usual spot where he would beat our mom there in the corner of the kitchen. He pinned me between the wall, the dark brown cabinets, the rolling dishwasher locked firmly into place with the extra-large microwave on top of it. I couldn't help but wonder what demons were in that corner that made him feel so powerful there.

This day was different, though. I was really angry and hurting—physically and emotionally. Possibly these were the raging hormones of a teenage girl. Or I was just reaching the breaking point for the cruelty-filled bullshit at home. As my brother and sister stood watch, he pinned me against the back door by the throat and told me this was the same as me hitting my little brother. This was his way of saying I shouldn't be picking or beating on those younger or weaker than myself. (This is probably the only truth my father ever spoke.)

As he held me there, I remember thinking to myself that I could kill this man in this moment with my bare hands. And, oh, how I wanted to. It would put us all out of our misery once and for all. Then, as I looked past him at my brother and sister crying, begging him not to hurt me, it was at that moment that I began to think about how our mother must have felt in this same situation all those times before. Pinned in that same spot. Literally, between a rock and a hard place.

She had to have felt helpless to fight back. Not because of a lack of strength, or will, or desire. More because she had the strength not to slaughter the father of her children in front of her children. Children who might not fully understand yet. How could she possibly explain that by killing him, she was saving them? Not to mention the fact that she too would be leaving us then, as they hauled her off to jail for killing the neighborhood miracle/saint.

I wasn't afraid of going to jail. That seemed like a nice reprieve. I was afraid my brother and sister would hate me, and I was certain my mom would hate me for killing him. After all, why else would she stay by his side all this time?

By this time, my sister had secretly called our mother. Mom came crashing through the door to find me still pinned against the back door and my brother and sister crying, screaming as they ran toward her. He put me down then and began screaming at her about how all of this was her fault and how he was teaching me a lesson about beating up on people smaller than me as he swung at her.

Mom took the beating that day, but I knew that beating was meant for me.

In truth, I am surprised he stopped with her and didn't come after me again. Then again, he was half a man now since the accident. As if he were ever a real man.

It was the last beating she would take in that basic, beige, godforsaken house.

Finally, A Divorce

♥

After that beating, Mom filed for divorce—finally. But that set into motion a whole new level of abuse and hate, even for my psychopathic father. I am not sure how she saw it playing out in her mind, but obviously, whatever she envisioned was not how it went down.

Once she had filed, she got a call from a neighbor saying dad and his brother, Tommy, had a U-Haul truck backed up to the house and were loading all of the furniture into the truck. Mom came to the school and checked all three of us out of our classes. We went home to find them and the truck gone, along with all of the furniture. Even our beds. What kind of father takes his children's beds? Maybe he was thinking of taking us too? Maybe that's the wounded mind of an abused child thinking/wanting to believe they mattered to such a sick human.

Not to mention, there was no fucking way we were going to choose staying with him over staying with Mom.

Mom loaded us all into the car, and we went to the bank. The bastard had also cleaned out all of the bank accounts. He probably did that first. Their business accounts (regardless of any checks still outstanding), their personal accounts, and our tiny savings accounts. She had $20 in her purse. She called the grandparents and asked for a loan. I remember thinking I never wanted anyone on my bank accounts ever again. Mom bought a pack of cigarettes and started smoking 'em. It was the first time I had ever seen her smoke. I was just fifteen, my sister thirteen, and my brother ten.

My brother took the split the hardest and assumed it was all his fault because of the few days before Mom had filed. He couldn't really seem to grasp what was happening. And, obviously, it was all our fault. I knew it was going to get worse before it got better, but maybe with dad out of the picture, we had a fighting chance now.

Feeling more vulnerable than ever, though, we had now reached critical-threat level. I also knew there was no way I could protect any of us from him or his minions. I was just a fucking child. I'm not sure when I took on that responsibility, but in those moments, I had no doubt it was mine and mine alone.

In all honesty, it's probably one of the biggest reasons I never had children of my own. I couldn't protect the children that weren't mine. Hell, I couldn't protect myself! Especially not from the predators inside my own home. How could it possibly be okay for me to bring another human being into this world, knowing this? It seemed like the most selfish act I could ever do would be to bring another human being into this shithole of a life.

The next few years were filled with court dates, people putting sugar in our gas tanks and taking the spark plugs out of our cars, and flat tires at least once a week.

The psychological warfare was equally as brutal. We received calls in the middle of the night, threatening us. He went so far as to have people call the house in the middle of the night, telling us they had been watching us, and threatening to kill us. We thought we were being clever when we would reply back that they didn't even know what we were wearing and could never find us. They would then describe our action-figure pajamas in detail and then describe the location of our separate bedrooms and the decor. Psychological warfare at its best. Thanks, dad. It is truly no wonder we were fucked up. *The Art of War* had nothing on our childhood or our psychopathic father.

Anytime there was a court date, dad would show up in his full back brace and arm crutches, pretending to still be crippled even though he could walk without even a cane. He would spew lies about how Mom was the one torturing him, cheating on him, and how she was the cold and callous one. These were the tactics I knew he or his family would use if I had killed him years ago. He was playing on the sympathy of the unknowing sheep of our tiny community.

Although I couldn't help but wonder if they would have done anything if they knew what a psychopath we had to live with day in and day out. Did anyone even really care?

We, as the children, were not allowed to testify. I feel sure dad didn't want that in case we said something we shouldn't. Although truth be told, we were all still scared to death of him. Dad made this sound as if he was looking out for our best interests and took advantage of this leverage anytime Mom's weak attorney tried to push back. Plus, dad, his latest girlfriend, Martha, and their henchmen would show up at my mom's office and beat her black and blue each time he "lost" in court. It was a cruelty-filled, never-waking nightmare— wondering what was going to happen next, not being able to take a deep breath knowing it might lead to "them" finding you. It was a less-than-fantastic time in high school for me, middle school for my brother and sister.

Even dad's sisters got in on trying to sway us children in his favor. They would come by to tell us what a piece of shit our mother was and how we would be better off with dear old dad. I often wondered how much abuse they had to endure to be so much in his favor. Fear was clearly their motivation.

During all of these court proceedings, we never knew if Mom was coming home. Or if he had killed her, and we just didn't know it yet. Much like his accident. Instability was an understatement.

We also never knew what kind of mess would be waiting for us each evening or each morning. We waited to see what the latest torture tactic, psychological attack, or physical attack would hold . . . or if he was just going to kill us in our sleep and be done with it. Nah, that would take his fun away.

There are studies now that compare this level of trauma for children with soldiers who come home with PTSD. The researchers should have just asked me. I could have confirmed that for them. It took decades for me to work through the feeling of expecting someone to come kill me at my father's behest. Decades of therapy to release that fight-or-flight response. Decades of therapy to not keep looking over my shoulder and panic if something that was out of the ordinary happened.

I think this is where the OCD comes into play. Everything must line up and be exactly *this* way, or that meant something was wrong. It meant something bad was about to happen. It meant prepare for war, prepare to fight for your life—not just a little old bar fight. Nope, things out of order meant load both barrels. In fact, load everything within reach, sharpen the knives, the spears, prep the food and water, get the masks ready—in those moments, this was the intense reality of the level of my trauma as a child. The stress level during these years kept me super skinny. Almost sickly skinny. Much like my aunt who was married to the pedo . . .

During one of the court dates, the judge ordered my dad to bring back all of the stuff he and Uncle Tommy stole. They never did. Instead, on the next court date, they both got on the stand and testified that Mom and two men came and picked up everything. This was a bald-faced lie. Martha, dad, and the henchmen had shown up for the regular beating after the judge told them to return the items. At least they were consistent.

During another episode at the office, after beating Mom, they took all of the records for the business. Every box, every piece of paper. They emptied the filing cabinets. They took everything. Totally wrecked the office. On the next court date, dad's attorney asked Mom to produce all of those documents that were stolen. No wonder I believe in conspiracy theories. #conspiracy

At seventeen, my senior year of high school, the divorce was final. During those two years prior, I believed no one and even went so far as to check the bank signatures. All of it led back to my dad and Martha, who had forged signatures and stolen almost all evidence to the contrary. May god have mercy on their souls.

As I contemplated suicide often during those two years and had wild, vivid, and really scary dreams, for the most part, I was alone. I couldn't help thinking that maybe if I died now, my mother, brother, and sister could possibly be saved from whatever bad stuff was coming next. Or at least I wouldn't be here to see it, feel it, and know I could do nothing about it.

I wasn't smart enough to know about pills or drugs, really, not yet. But I did know about guns and knives. I could just go into the bathroom and slit my wrists in the tub like they do in the movies. No one would check on me for hours because no one really cared anyway; at least that's how it felt. Or, better yet, I could go "play" in the woods behind the house and do it there. Maybe the animals would finish me off, and no one would ever have to know.

My dreams were mostly fighting my dad or his brother or someone he sent over to harass us. Of course, with my tiny frame and emotions filled with rage, in the dreams they easily took me over and killed me . . . or worse. Sometimes, the dreams were straight out of the last horror movie we had watched. Blood everywhere, everyone dead, except the killer who walks free and clear without a trace and onto his next victim. Either way, at least I would be dead, and it would be over for me. On a side note, I don't watch horror movies or even scary movies to this day.

No one knew. My best friend, Trena, and maybe the neighbors had an inkling—but not really. And no one ever stepped in to help. No one would know. No one would even care if I had died then. They would just go on fighting, and I would (sort of) be at peace. Every day was just another slap in the face and another psychological stabbing for my brother, my sister, and me.

My mom, while she obviously had been through hell with us, was in her own mess. During those years, I remember her telling us children, "If you wouldn't have made it here when you did, I would have never had y'all." She had gotten pregnant with me when she was just seventeen and still in high school.

She often reminded me that I was the reason they were even together. That was a lot of weight on my tiny shoulders. If I hadn't been born, my brother and sister would have never had to endure the abuse from our father. Those times, I wished I had never been born. I know now she had no idea how heavily those words weighed on me. After all, her own mother probably said the same things to her. It is just how it goes for us eldest daughters, bearing the burdens of the generations. As with all the generations before.

We also knew that dad's family considered Mom "white trash," and they made sure she and us kids knew it every chance they got. They treated us as if we were lepers with extra-incurable cooties that might rub off on them if they touched us or even looked in our direction. Our dad's mom would make us sit away from the others during mealtime. And if we were ever beyond eyesight of her, she would check on us every five minutes or so. As if to let us know we couldn't be trusted. It also kept us on edge around her and our dad's family.

At that time, we had no idea the hell Mom endured growing up. Maybe marrying our dad was somehow better than where she was coming from? Maybe she was still afraid of what would happen if she told. #metoo

During my senior year of high school, Trena and I were looking at apartments and planned to get full-time jobs as soon as we had graduated. It was a way out of this hell, and I knew my best friend would allow my brother and sister to stay with us.

I also wanted to take auto mechanics my senior year of high school. Keep in mind, I was already working two jobs and helping take care of my brother and sister. Mom said no and made me enroll in aerobics class instead. I was furious. So, I quit one of my jobs and took a job at the full-service gas station near the house. It was all fun and games until some older man pulled into the full-service lane and refused to allow me to even help. He said he didn't want some girl touching his car. His wife sat there in the front seat without a word. I still learned to change a tire, plug a tire, change oil, and use a few extra cuss words I hadn't heard before. I also invited this derelict group working with me at the gas station home for Thanksgiving dinner, much to my mother's dismay. Grandma was there that year, too. I mean, it was my Christianly thing to do, right? They had no place to go. They were single guys mostly with family far away from this place, but they were all nice to me and watched out for me; they felt like family.

Much more happened during those years, and once in a while, it was good stuff. My plan was still to get the hell out of there as soon as possible. I had been working two jobs since the divorce: our neighbor helped me get a job at Burger King, and his wife helped me get a paper route.

Working my two jobs and paying for most of my own things already, plus some of my brother and sister's necessary items, I felt confident I could make it on my own. The great debate during my senior year was about the graduation invitations. I had to pay for however many I was going to send out, so the list was very, very short. After all, there was no one celebrating me or my life, anyway.

Fuck them.

My friends at school and my mom all said I should "invite everyone" because they give you gifts—usually cash—for graduation. These assholes have never even called me on my birthday or Christmas. What made them think they would show up now to celebrate me? *Whatever*, I thought. *I'll do as I'm told. But only because I can see the light showing me my path out of this fucking bullshit.*

I paid for my own class ring and all of the invitations, even the ones I sent to dear old dad and his family. As suspected, there were no acknowledgements, there was no cash, and there were no gifts of any kind from any of them. None of them showed up for my graduation.

My effort was a total waste of my money and time and a clear indication of the power my mother held over me—even though I couldn't see that then.

As graduation came and went, Mom decided we were moving to Atlanta in August. Her boyfriend had accepted a job there, and she decided that a new place would be best for us all.

I told her I wasn't going. I was moving out with Trena as soon as the summer was over. Just after graduation and before her big announcement of moving to Atlanta, Mom told me I could not live with her if I wasn't going to school unless I paid rent, even just for the summer. I remember feeling then that she clearly didn't give a shit about me, or she would have given me this tiny fucking break of a summer so I could work my ass off and make something of myself. Make something of myself to escape this prison she had created for all of us.

In this moment, I made a mental note that no one was ever going to give me any breaks in this life. After all, my own mother won't give me any. Maybe I didn't deserve any since I didn't kill him when I had the chance. Or maybe it was because

I beat up my little brother, or because I told them about my uncle, or, or, or . . . the list could go on for decades.

Now, knowing that I wasn't planning to move with her to Georgia, Mom sent in the big guns.

Grandma.

Being the first grandchild, my grandparents could do no wrong in my eyes. At least back then. Prior to that one summer with the bad uncle, I felt they saw me for the shining star I could be if I could ever get out from under the weight of my family situation. That was obviously not the truth, but that's what I needed to believe at that time.

Grandma came down to the coast, asked me to go for a walk with her, and gave me a talking to. You know, the one about how I had to go with them to "protect them." Now we know where that bullshit started.

My tiny shoulders had been burdened with that task by the one person I trusted most in all the world at that time: Grandma. Having overlooked her treatment and response to the uncle incident, she was the one person I had left, the only one who I felt sort-of cared for me. In hindsight, maybe it was self-preservation on her part—or this was just what daughters were supposed to do, and it was the matriarch's job to make sure it happened. And after all, if Grandma said it, it must be true, right?

We all moved to Atlanta in August of that year.

Brighter Than The Sun / The Son

♥

I was eighteen, my sister was fifteen, and my brother was twelve. Though we had all moved to Georgia, my brother went back and forth between Georgia and Mississippi. He was struggling, I suppose, to find his own path. I was of age now, and it was time for me to go to work. Maybe school, too, but definitely work. We saw our first real "snow" that year, in Georgia, although it was just a dusting of snow for the seasoned Georgian.

My brother's behavior became a little more erratic each time he returned from our dad's and Mississippi. By the time he turned eighteen, just five short years later, it was apparent he was fighting his own demons, which we knew nothing about.

Over the first few years in Georgia, my brother and sister were dabbling in drugs and heavy on the alcohol. Not that I would notice. I was headed toward freedom. They could come if they wanted, but we were on our own now. After all, we were all adults. Besides, in my eyes, my little brother could do no wrong. He was smooth-talking, tall, handsome, and a truly gentle soul. We had nicknamed him "Fresh Prince" after the character Will Smith played in the sitcom. He was quick-witted, funny, and seemed truly unstoppable. Life was going to be amazing for him, and I couldn't wait to see what he did in this life. We were going to watch and laugh from the sidelines. I just knew it to be true!

I remember my little brother as this skinny, smiling boy with beautiful blonde curls swooping up from his neck, always walking around with a glass of sweet tea in his hand. His infectious laugh, quick wit, comfortable smile, and gentle, kind heart were visible from the moment he showed up in this world. At times, his blonde hair looked like a halo in the Mississippi sun. He seemed so unafraid of the world, and I wanted to be in that energy every possible moment.

Maybe everyone else did too because he had a lot of friends growing up, unlike my sister or myself. He was an average student but always seemed to date the prettiest girls. He sort of played tennis during junior high and high school. Football kind of waned after elementary school. He wasn't in the band, not part of the "smart club," but he was somehow a part of the popular crowd.

He seemed so unafraid of anything, really! Willing to try things without a hint of the self-conscious insecurities that plagued me. I remember that one time, our aunt Cathy came down to the coast and took the three of us for a walk. We were talking about edible bugs and plants around us when Aunt Cathy picked up a roly-poly and told us they were delicious with a glint in her eye. She pretended to toss it into her mouth but actually had tossed it over her shoulder. My brother immediately reached down, picked one up, and actually ate it! Aunt Cathy wasn't fast enough to stop him and told him to spit it out. He was still chewing that bug. We laughed and laughed.

He said, "It wasn't too bad, and I didn't die."

That is one of my favorite memories of Aunt Cathy, too. She died at a young age in a car accident. Seems many of my living guides in this life left me too soon.

That cream-colored brick house we grew up in was ranch-style, and we liked to climb onto the roof. As many kids in those days, we were just that bored, I guess. Bobby was always willing to give my sister and me a boost up onto the rooftop, too. Even at a young age, he was taller than either of us, and we all liked to sit up on the roof and look out over the neighborhood. We could sit up there for hours just talking about life. He kept us laughing the whole time. Time passed so quickly though we were doing absolutely nothing.

Dinnertime was especially interesting. The three of us worked better together during dinner clean-up than at any other time. We were on a mission to avoid having to eat the foods we didn't like while also avoiding beatings or no food at all, depending on dad's mood that evening. We had these old aluminum glasses, and we each had our own designated color. The glasses were purple, green/blue, and a weird yellow color. I can't remember what each of our colors was, but the idea was to avoid fighting over whose glass was whose.

Our dad was big on meat, mostly gristle-filled ribeye steaks from the meat delivery service, cooked to death like hockey pucks. We all three hated those—a common ground to begin our collaboration. There was usually some type of potatoes and a vegetable with each meal. Bobby didn't like most vegetables, and none of us liked the gristle from the steaks. Dad would not allow you to spit out the gristle from the steak once you had chewed the meat off. You had to swallow it all.

The three of us usually had to do the dishes after dinner. Our plan was pretty ingenious for our ages; we would pretend to take a sip of our tea and spit the "gross" food into our tea glasses. After dinner, we could dispose of the contents, usually with Bobby making a joke about needing to "water the plants" outside, where he promptly dumped the food remnants from our glasses for the critters to enjoy. At least the food didn't go to waste, right?

As my brother approached eighteen, we began to notice that his behavior had changed dramatically. He left Atlanta and went to stay with our dad. We didn't know he wouldn't be living with dad. Instead, he was living with a girl, and they were dealing acid, pot, LSD, and anything else. Most likely, they only sold whatever was left of their stash that they didn't do themselves.

His girlfriend was bad news. Dad knew it and never said a fucking word. Not saying my brother was innocent here, just that it was a path he knew nothing about before she arrived. They were living in a run-down fourplex on the not-so-safe side of town. On some level, it was pretty smart of him to live close to his customers . . . but also dangerous.

One summer, a short time after he moved, dad did call with a cry for help, saying that Bobby was "out of control." If our psychopathic asshole of a sperm donor father was saying he was out of control, there was no doubt it was a shit show of a situation. We could be walking into anything at this point. Mom and I immediately left Atlanta and drove straight to Mississippi.

Mom and I talked on the way down, formulating a plan to "rescue" my brother. But we had no idea what we could be walking into. We weren't even sure what we were rescuing him from, or if he would agree to be rescued at all. He was over eighteen now. We worried the whole way, playing out scenarios of what would happen, which part each of us would play, and who else would be involved. Although we forgot to play it out far enough to see what would happen once we got him back to Atlanta, assuming we even made it that far.

We knew we were going to stay with Ms. Jackie. She and Mom had been friends since my sister was in elementary school. Ms. Jackie had two daughters of her own and was raising them as a single mom. I am not sure if Mom ever told her how bad it was with our dad, but I always wondered.

Ms. Jackie was also the only adult who ever asked me how I was doing during those dad years before the divorce and even after the divorce. All of the other adults were super concerned about my brother and sister, which makes sense because they were still so young, cute, and somewhat innocent and still friendly. I was already a hardened ball of nerves, edgy, non-trusting, and very angry. Over those years, Ms. Jackie and I formed a special bond that could never be broken, and one Mom could never understand and sometimes seemed jealous about. I felt safe going to Ms. Jackie's, especially not knowing what circus awaited us with our dad and my brother.

We arrived late that night to Mississippi. Mom and Ms. Jackie stayed up talking. I went to bed, exhausted from the trip and the emotional rollercoaster but also anticipating that I would be doing all of the heavy lifting come morning.

We got up early, had coffee with Ms. Jackie, and talked through our plan once more. Extract my brother, pack his stuff, and head back to Atlanta. It seemed simple enough, right? What could go wrong?

We found my brother. He was out of his mind, hopped up on something. He wanted nothing to do with us. He said he really just wanted to sleep. The electricity in the apartment had been turned off—for how long, we weren't sure. His girlfriend had left him, and although the apartment was still full of her things, she was nowhere to be found. Remember that plan to take him and his things back to Atlanta? Now we could add getting him cleaned up to that list.

Good luck with that bullshit.

Now that my brother was safely at Ms. Jackie's and sleeping, it was time for the real work. How could that sweet, curly-haired blonde boy have turned into an aimless, lifeless monster? "Monster" might have been too strong in the beginning, but I struggle with articulating the unraveling of this beautiful human in any other way. He went from the kid who would run across the street to help someone carry their groceries to a sarcastic punk who would laugh in your face when you asked for help. He was angrier, too, as if the psychological beatings of our childhood were finally coming to the surface for him. I knew this pain all too well.

As the eldest daughter of the eldest daughter of the eldest daughter, I know that's how this shit works—you're expected to just handle it, whatever *it* is. That doesn't even matter, and you shouldn't worry your pretty little head about it. Just get the shit done. No one cares how you do it or how you're feeling about it. This was a message I was all too familiar with, and back then—like a good soldier—I always carried out my orders.

Now that we had my brother and he was safe, it was time to go get his things. I was elected to go to his dark, stinky apartment, which smelled of smoke, stale booze, and rotten food, to collect his things. I took what I might need—boxes, trash bags, gloves—and got an order to take what I knew for sure was his and leave the rest.

Just as I had entered his apartment and began bagging his clothes, my asshole father and his even-more-of-an-asshole older brother, Tommy, pulled up in two separate vehicles. My father said my mom had called him and told him I might need some help getting Bobby's things.

I was so mad I could have spit nails clearing a thousand cornfields. How could she possibly think this was a good idea? She knew how much I hated that sorry asshole. And then to add his my-way-or-the-highway brother, too? What in the actual fuck!?

As if there wasn't enough pressure to get this done quickly and without going to jail for having to "hurt, maim, or seriously injure" some random druggie looking for a fix. We had no idea if Bobby and his girlfriend owed his supplier money or someone else money or if their clients were coming to the apartment. We had no fucking idea. I was already on heightened alert: shoulders at my ears, knife in my boot . . . you know, just in case. And then add these two mother fuckers to my stress level. Thanks, Mom. #badass #handlethatshit

Tommy was already fucking half-lit on booze, maybe other stuff—who the fuck knows for sure. I do know it was 9:30 in the fucking morning! I asked them to just wait outside, "to keep watch," which, thankfully, they did. Mostly. Tommy was all too eager to "help" with my brother's guns, tools, and fishing equipment.

"I'll take these for safekeeping," he said. Rolling my eyes, I knew my brother would never see his guns, tools, or fishing gear ever again.

I went back to work loading my brother's clothes into big, black plastic garbage bags with each piece reeking of cigarettes, vomit, and booze. My brother never stood a chance with these two fuckers as examples of what a man was supposed to be.

At one point, my father yelled to me how much he appreciated me "taking care of my brother." That fucking asshole. *He was supposed to be living with you,* I thought. *You are the motherfucker who should have been taking care of him. Not out here with some two-bit tramp dealing drugs.*

"Thanks for being such a great parent," I'd mumble under my breath, knowing he couldn't hear me since he was a good fifty yards from the door. Fucker.

As I was carrying the last of the bags to the car, Tommy stood at the door of the apartment and wouldn't let me pass. I was holding heavy ass bags, nearly vomiting from the smell. I knew he had already downed at least another six-pack while he loaded my brother's guns, tools, and fishing gear.

He had the audacity to say to me, "Do you think you should be doing this since she isn't here? I'd be mad if somebody did this to me." Then added, "This must be hard for you. Let me give you a hug."

Are you fucking kidding me right now? You and dear old dad out there cleaned out my childhood home less than a decade ago without a single regret or thought about me, my brother, or my sister. Fuck you, motherfucker. You don't know shit!

GET THE FUCK OUT OF MY WAY, YOU DRUNK, NASTY FUCKING PERV!

I DO NOT WANT A HUG FROM YOU NOW OR EVER!

He didn't move, though. He stood there. As I stared into his soulless, black eyes, I knew there were only two ways out that door—drop the bags, hug him, pick the bags back up, and be on my way. Or slit his fucking throat, gut him like the nasty fucking pig that he is, and hang him out on the porch. As a reminder for all of these motherfuckers to know that I was not someone to be fucked with. I kept thinking about the knife in my boot and which way would be the easiest and fastest way to get to it. Flashes of his blood splattered everywhere. The best would be the priceless look on my dad's face, watching me gut his brother in front of him. I bet that motherfucker would have gotten in his truck and ran like the coward he was.

Fuck these motherfuckers.

Sweaty, angry, dirty, hurt, confused—did I mention angry?—I dropped the bags, hugged him, and went about my business of "taking care of my brother."

Handle that shit. Those were my orders. Not gutting cowards out on the front porch.

In hindsight, maybe my mother's control over me back then saved me from prison. At least there's that.

By the time I got back to Ms. Jackie's, I was raging mad. I asked my mother what the fuck she was doing calling those two assholes. She apologized and said she was worried about me being there by myself. *Fine, whatever. I need a shower.* As always, I was handling the dirty bombs, deflecting the bullshit, all while my sweet little brother, Bobby, slept peacefully. Guess this is how I saw my life, anyway. Always taking care of shit while everyone else rested. They were relaxed and at ease, knowing I would always show up, I would always be there to just handle it . . .

As we traveled back to Atlanta the next day, my brother began telling us about his life. Mom and I both sat quietly, trying not to gasp at the horrific shit he was spewing. Bar fights, drugs, running from the cops . . . for fuck's sake, he was just a kid, and where the fuck had our father been? Once back in Atlanta, we didn't think he would have such easy access to the drugs. Maybe things would start to level out for him now. How naïve were we? First thing, though, was to wash those fucking clothes. I still wanted to puke—that's how bad the smell was.

It took nearly a month to get him cleaned up and sober. He got a job at the local grocery store, close enough to walk to work. After less than a month, he was fired because his boss said he "scared the customers." He was also scaring us. He would go into uncontrollable laughter at odd moments and begin spouting Bible verses, saying, "Nebuchadnezzar said it's time for all of us to die." And then he would laugh and laugh in this weird, eerie tone.

Although the names from the Bible verses would change, these outbursts became a regular occurrence. He would tell us wild stories that weren't anything he had experienced in this lifetime. It was hard to watch and even scarier to leave my mother alone with him under those circumstances.

My mother recalls times alone with him that were scary and frustrating for her without any of us there, before we got out of bed, or after we had gone to sleep.

Back then, she still had the morning paper delivered. During one of my brother's episodes where he had been up all night, he would not allow her to go out and get the morning paper because he was convinced it was a bomb someone had thrown into the yard. He blocked the door to her bedroom and wouldn't allow her to leave her room. Another time, he

locked her out of the house and followed her around to each
door in the house, locking them before she could come back
inside. On a separate occasion, he had decided she was the
enemy and kicked her—hard, in the stomach. No matter what,
she never allowed any of us to intervene, and we followed her
lead on his care and treatment. We knew it was out of love and
compassion.

Besides, what could we do?

By now, I was determined to be a millionaire by thirty,
defeating the male-dominated monopoly in the insurance
industry in the big city of Atlanta. This small-town girl was
about to teach those fuckers just who they were dealing with.
So what if I had been told my whole life I was stupid? And that
I was a piece of shit and would never amount to anything?
Consider the source when you hear such bullshit. I wasn't
falling for that. I was working hard every day—and I just *knew*
I would make it.

Soon, my brother seemed to level out a bit. We assumed
the drugs were finally leaving his system. We were thankful
and also hopeful that this was a turning point for him. We had
no idea he had found a supplier for pot, and that was his way
back to sanity in those fleeting moments.

He liked to go to the bars and play pool and had become
somewhat of a pool shark—you know, the kind with his own
pool cue, hustling all of the suckers at the local bars. He was
really good, too. He could get into the bars at eighteen in
Atlanta. Often he called me to tell me to come down to the
bars because he needed a partner. I didn't want to. I was on
a mission toward success. He would usually talk me into it,
though. I am pretty sure that kid could sell ice to Eskimos.

Sometimes, he would call and tell me he had hustled the wrong people and needed my help. I always showed up for him.

I should mention here that I totally suck at playing pool. After a few beers, I could get out of my own way enough to shoot a decent game but nothing like my brother's fancy "English on the ball" style. He taught me how to play 8 Ball and 9 Ball and tried to teach me how to put some "English on the ball." That last one never took.

My brother and I had some great laughs during those days. He would always tell me to order a Bud Light—I hated that beer then, and I hate it now. But I did it anyway. I wasn't going to be drinking it; he was. I needed to be sober in case shit got crazy. I was there to save my brother, not drink or enjoy myself.

At some point, my brother met a really great lady who was a single mom of two young girls. He seemed to straighten out more with her around, thankfully. She was good for him, and we all loved her and her daughters. Bobby got a job at a local car dealership, and they moved in together.

Ahhh, stable . . . until it wasn't.

Over the few years he had been with us in Atlanta, we would struggle with my brother going back and forth from reality to hallucinating far, far from reality. My mother and I took him in for a psychological evaluation at around twenty-two years of age, where he was diagnosed with paranoid schizophrenia.

He was prescribed Haldol for the "voices." We didn't know then that this medication would turn him into, basically, a zombie. Worse, it would turn him into a hollowed-out human being, with shakes similar to what you'd see with Parkinson's disease, unable to comprehend simple things. Then, they would add more medication to control the side effects. That's when we started looking into alternative medicine, holistic healing, and the human body.

We started with alternatives for the Haldol and the Parkinson's medications they had given him. This is where my adventure into the human body and healing began. We started giving him doses of vitamins and supplements. Lots and lots of supplements. More than the usual dose of all of the B's. Definitely some D and E. And a shit ton of amino acids and a multivitamin, because he still hated vegetables.

Mom and I began to see some improvement and continued our research each night at the bar in the upstairs kitchen. With its mauve and country-blue walls, decor, rugs, stove burner covers, and seat cushions. Gosh, I hated those colors.

Mom and I poured over library books on his condition, researched the internet as much as our knowledge would allow, and into what was considered, at that time, "alternative" healing and wellness. He was still taking the Haldol and Parkinson's meds, too. We weren't comfortable enough with the progress to have the doctors wean him off those just yet.

When my brother noticed within himself that he was feeling better, he decided, on his own, to stop the Haldol. In fact, he stopped everything: all of the pharmaceutical medicines as well as the supplements. Cold turkey. We, too, had become so comfortable with his progress that we didn't notice he had stopped taking everything.

We got a phone call that he was in jail. He had been arrested after leaving his vehicle in the middle of the road—in the turn lane, outside of a convenience store, where he had assaulted the clerk in an attempt to steal cigarettes. He didn't need to steal; he had money and cigarettes at home. He was lost in his hallucinations again after only a few days off the meds and supplements. In an effort to provide a smaller world—Gulfport, Mississippi over Atlanta, Georgia—we took him to my father's house in Gulfport. That was the worst mistake of our entire lives. And of his.

My funny, vibrant, halo of curly blonde hair brother had just turned twenty-four that April. That same year, he died from a self-inflicted gunshot wound while in the "care" of our father. He left us—me—forever on October 18, 1998.

More than twenty years after his death, I can still see his bright-as-sunshine halo and his curl-framed face.

I can still hear his mischievous laughter.

Anonymous

Tough Love

♥

I Wish I could tell you his death was the only one during that decade. But our family trauma had begun a few years before my brother's death. The short version is that we had moved to Atlanta, to a place where I could see possibilities for myself and for my brother and sister. Hell, even for my mom!

Bobby's death was in 1998, so I am going to go back about five years.

Working different jobs as a young girl with a thick Mississippi accent and a high school diploma was not the easiest in the big city of Atlanta, to be sure. I wanted to fit in so badly. I would have probably tried anything back then! This town meant freedom! I could smell it and feel it as it rushed through my very soul!

One of my first jobs through a temp agency was as a receptionist for Paymaster Checkwriter. Back in the days before there was fancy paper for checks, this was the answer to security measures for corporate checks. I made $9.00 an hour. I was so excited that I told *everybody* how much I made.

Before that, it was minimum wage at Burger King. I had never had such wealth flowing my way. I just knew I was onto something here.

On one of our trips back home to visit, we stopped by my grandparents', and I told them how much I was making at my new, fancy job in the big city of Atlanta. My grandmother informed me that she wasn't even making that much after twenty years at "the plant." I felt sad and vindicated and also guilty for the vindication. Sad because she obviously wasn't valued at her job, even after twenty years. Vindicated that I was on the "right" path but also guilty that somehow this meant I was saying what they provided for us wasn't good enough.

I think this is how my mom saw it, too. Right about then, she probably wished she hadn't had Grandma convince me to move with her to Atlanta.

I dabbled at a few different colleges and jobs in those first few years, including business school and fashion and modeling school. The hours for fashion school weren't conducive to full-time employment, which was required to live the lifestyle of the big city girl I was becoming. So, I quit school and went to work full-time. I did, however, participate in a few modeling gigs and even a beauty pageant! I won Miss Congeniality. I was also a cocktail waitress, a bartender, and a medical secretary.

I had also fallen in love. I was sort of working, sort of going to school, sort of playing at modeling, and he just let me play. Right up until I said we should get married.

That was when he told me I needed to "pick a direction and stick with it" before we could even consider settling down. In hindsight, I don't think he meant it the way I took it, but I guess we will never know. To me, he was saying to pick anything and go with it if I wanted to settle down. But I think what he was saying was to keep playing until I found something I wanted to "settle down" with. Who knows for sure, and it doesn't even matter anymore because I chose then, and I have been in that industry for thirty-plus years now.

Once I picked that direction and started to run with it, that's about the time my brother's life started falling apart. The direction I chose offered me long-term solutions to my foreseeable "problems," including unlimited potential in the financial arena as well as an opportunity to make my mark on this world.

Hell yeah! I AM IN!

Among those part-time jobs was one as a data entry clerk for an insurance brokerage house. So, I went to the boss and asked if I could go full-time. He said "absolutely," and away I went. I met some truly wonderful people on that journey who taught me a whole lot about life, love, liberty, and the pursuit of happiness.

One of them, Doug, who is still a lifelong friend, for some reason unbeknownst to me took it upon himself to teach me to speak "properly." It is funny to me now, but I am sure it was not funny back then. I so desperately wanted to shed that tattered rag of Mississippi cloaked so tightly around my neck, but I had no idea how or where to begin looking!

Doug suggested I watch the old Audrey Hepburn movie *My Fair Lady*. At the time, and even years later, I had no idea why, although it was a great movie and still remains one of my favorites. Doug would correct my grammar as I spoke, even in front of others. He and I had an odd zig-zag kind of relationship, work partners, best friends, lovers, mischief-makers, drinking buddies, and skinny-dipping renegades. I say zig-zag because we were all over the map and always seemed to miss opportunities to take our relationship to any other meaningful place. That old saying about "a reason, a season" comes to mind, but I am thankful for more than one season with my dear friend Doug.

With my true love, Jon, came many dear friends, too. One of his best friends, Louis (Lou), is an amazing human and, as it turns out, another lifelong friend of mine. Jon, Lou, Jimmy, Matt, Patrick, Darrin, Geno, Mike, Stacey, Melinda, Teresa, Michael, and a few others whose faces I can see but names escape me—the group of us would sit for hours, drinking, playing cards, talking, and laughing until the wee hours of the morning.

Lou brightened up every room with a great big smile and a tight hug. A truly genuine human being. This group was wild, fun, and spontaneous.

We decided to go to New Orleans for Halloween one year—all of us. We all dressed as cat burglars. We had so much fun, and if memory serves, there is a video somewhere of us doing cartwheels and doorway-to-doorway rolls, "sneaking" down the hallway of our hotel. So much laughter. Those were good days.

Lou and I used to play a game with new words, too. We would message each other with a "word of the day." I remember "plethora" and "panacea" were two of our favorites from those days. It was surprisingly fun when it wasn't attached to any sort of required learning. All of the fun, learning, love, and friendship was a stark reprieve from my Mississippi life, my mother, and my brother. A welcome and strongly desired reprieve.

Jon and I paired off, Mike and Melinda paired off, Darrin and Stacey paired off. Michael became my brother-in-law, marrying my sister and also the father of my favorite human in all the land.

A few others I am still friends with on social media. I have met Geno and his beautiful wife on my travels, but Lou—he has been the constant and probably the glue that holds the remainder of us together. I know Lou and I will be friends to the end, and I am truly thankful for him in this life. Thankful for showing me that these humans do have staying power and a deep love that is everlasting.

This is where my story gets a little wonky. In pushing for marriage with Jon, most likely as an escape from my ever-tightening, heavy, rusting chains of Mississippi, we hit a couple of snags, even though I'd chosen a direction and was pursuing the insurance route. Eventually, we did marry. This left Mom and my brother alone in her house as we moved into our own home just a few months after our marriage. Over the course of our year-long engagement, my sister became pregnant even though she was told she could never have children due to a plethora of uterine fibroids. Lots of "never gonna happen," happened. And in short order.

Just one month before my wedding date, Bobby had one of his "episodes."

My sister went into labor that night after the stress of the episode.

As I write this piece of my life, reviewing all of the other pieces, it is no wonder anything less than total chaos feels uncomfortable to me. It's as if I'm always waiting for the next plate to shatter. If there aren't a ridiculous number of plates spinning, then something is about to happen—and it won't be good. If there is calm, there is a storm coming, and make no mistake, you will owe penance for this calm, and this will be a mighty and terrible storm for sure. Strictly as punishment!

Distancing myself from that chaos was like trying to bathe a cat in the tub. Claws out, spine stiffened, hissing and biting. And, sadly, that's how I have been for the majority of my life.

When my brother started really regressing into the abyss, the storm of my own life was already upon us. I was wrapped in my own world, biting and clawing to escape the world that seemed to pull me—more like suck me—back in. Like a vicious tornado that just kept circling back to the same spot, looking for any missing pieces to destroy.

My thought patterns back then were hopeful: *If I just keep moving, the bad won't catch up with me. Or maybe it'll resolve itself, so I don't have to deal with it.*

For the second time in this book, good luck with that bullshit.

The sands of time were running and fast on my short-lived life. This was the fork in the road where I could pursue my own hopes and dreams or give them up to save my brother. It sounds so dramatic as I write it, but also brings tears of my truth at that time.

I chose myself. A choice that has haunted me since and may possibly forever.

Being in therapy, I was just learning about boundaries. We were also going to AA meetings, ANON meetings, and NA meetings with the help of another beautiful human named Phil, who agreed to sponsor my brother. Phil is an amazing, selfless human who helped my entire family during this tumultuous time. He was a trusted friend, confidant, and soother of fears. Phil always had a kind word, an offer of consolation, and was a truth speaker who would hold your hand while you walked through the hot holy hell that is addiction.

Mom and I also attended Tough Love meetings, counseling sessions, and doctor's appointments with and for ourselves and my brother. I felt I had done all that I could for him, especially after all that they were telling us in those meetings. He had to choose to help himself. Otherwise, our efforts were fruitless and only robbed us of energy and resources from our own lives. This kept our family in turmoil for many, many years.

Following the Tough Love strategy, I chose me. I chose my new family, my new life, and my new goals, dreams, and hopes for a better future with my new husband. Bed of roses, white picket fences, and wraparound porches—that was my destiny. Not this shit show of back and forth, push and pull, up and down, drama-filled, tear-soaked pillows weighted down with guilt and shame of a past that none of us could outrun, no matter how hard we tried.

My guilt from my brother's death has weighed on me since the day he left this plane. There is no amount of consolation that can ease that. I should have done something differently. Now I'm six blankets deep in guilt. At the end of my days, this will be the only true thing in this life (so far) that I will need to reconcile. There are so many other things I have done "wrong" or people I have hurt in this life, but this one . . . this one sinks me to my knees every time.

As his death struck me down into the abyss, I wished for death for the wrong I felt I had done to such a beautiful human. There were but a few who still stood close through those storms. I think, on some level, Jon tried as best he knew how, but our divorce was final just one month prior to my brother's death, so there were other concrete weights drowning him and me in this storm. Lou and Doug both stayed, too. Doug saved me on many a night as I cried myself to sleep, only to be awakened by the phone telling me it was only 9 o'clock, forcing me to go for long rides.

I am not sure any of those three ever knew the depth of my darkness. But I am thankful that they showed up and continued to stand by my side. I am sure it was not easy given my level of "crazy" on top of my current state of mind.

There was no doubt in my mind that the world would be a better place without me in it. At least, that's what I was thinking then. At least then, I wouldn't be able to disappoint another human or let another human go to the next plane on my watch.

I had seen what my brother's suicide had done to my mother and also how I felt about his suicide. Knowing this meant my own death would have to be an "accident." Those were just some of the spiraling thoughts that filled my days during those next two years after my brother's death. My hope was lost—stolen. Stolen by a decision to focus on my career, money, myself, my new family, and not those who needed me most and who had been in my life long before any of those other opportunities.

The decade of the nineties was a rough one for me, to be certain, but also a beautiful one with many surprises, happy moments, and progress. It was definitely a quid-pro-quo decade. One of those eighties boxing matches—hold-each other's opposing forearms and trading punches until someone dies kind of decade.

Only it was the nineties, and someone did die.

Six In Four

♥

My *favorite uncle died* from the hand of his own son. His coward of a son waited for him behind a door and shot him in cold blood. That fucker still brags about it to this day. The son was under eighteen, so Grandma lied—under oath—to save him from being tried as an adult, using the excuse that she didn't want to lose her son and her grandson all at once. The world would have been better off, but . . . hindsight, I guess. Uncle Billy was murdered in May of 1995.

Uncle Billy was my favorite for at least a thousand reasons. He was a total renegade badass who marched to the beat of his own drum. He was nine years older than me, so most of the time, he was more like a big brother. He had odd eating habits, too. As kids, we would watch him take a loaf of white bread, and then get a bowl or either barbeque sauce or yellow mustard, and use a slice of bread to sop up the sauce or mustard. Some days he finished a whole loaf of bread. It was gross and fascinating at the same time.

He also rode a motorcycle, an old Yamaha XS1100. Wish we still had that thing today. I have no doubt he and I would have been great riding partners as lifelong renegades on our motorcycles. His other vehicle was one of those old Yugos. That thing looked so out of place among the big farm trucks in Mississippi. Uncle Billy told us kids all kinds of stories about growing up. Some ghost stories, too. He also taught me to drive a stick shift. He was patient and cured every sad face with laughter. I'd like to think some of my own badassery comes from him.

By December of the same year, Grandpa was also dead. Grandpa had a spot on his forehead that had been growing for at least a decade. He finally went to the doctor and found out it was cancer. After a full check-up, Grandpa was diagnosed with lung cancer sometime in late summer. The family all went to Grandma's for Thanksgiving. Grandpa pulled me aside then and told me he wouldn't be alive by Christmas. I told him not to talk like that. He kept his word then and died December of '95, about a week before Christmas and barely two weeks after a full left pneumonectomy.

This one was particularly rough as this man hung the moon for me. I had learned all of that insurance lingo by now and explained it all to the family when the doctors talked about what was going to happen. Just a few short months prior to this diagnosis, some door-to-door salesman had come across my grandparents' place and convinced them to cancel their long-held cancer policies in favor of what he was selling.

"It's cheaper and pays more," he told them.

It was a lie.

Their policies were the ones they had before insurance companies realized the shit they had stepped into with those cancer policies. You know, the ones that paid *everything* if you were diagnosed, treated, or died from cancer. These new policies also had a waiting period that was not waived with their prior coverage.

After his diagnosis and subsequent death, my grandparents received nothing from this salesman, this policy, or his company. I am not sure if I ever told anyone then, but this is the real reason I became an insurance agent so many years ago. To do my part in putting an end to this type of thievery. Blatant lies that cost poor, uneducated folks their life savings and that of their families. Fucking bullshit, and I wish I knew that guy's name—wished I'd known it then and definitely wish I knew it now.

Thankfully, my grandparents also had a burial policy with the funeral home in addition to that shit policy they were sold by that snake oil salesman. We all went to the funeral home together to make the arrangements: Mom, Grandma, myself, Aunt Linda, and Uncle Paul. Jon also went with us, as he was already a part of the family even though we weren't married yet.

Once at the funeral home, though, everything fell to pieces. That's when the eldest daughter of the eldest daughter of the eldest daughter was required to step into her own "manhood"—without an explanation.

Grandma, Mom, Uncle Paul, and Aunt Linda started talking about something in hushed voices. After that, none of them wanted anything to do with making the arrangements for Grandpa. So I had to do it. I had to walk through with the funeral director, who had known me my whole life, although I couldn't tell you his name if my life depended on it. Sure, I was old enough and I had been through this process a few times, but never as the primary person. I picked out the casket, the cards, the whole deal, all the while looking over my shoulder at the four of them huddled, talking, and crying. I was brave then, even though it was not acknowledged by anyone. I held back my tears, squared my shoulders, and handled that shit like the badass that I am.

When the day came for the actual funeral service, that's when I lost it. It was all business as usual until they closed the casket.

When the service was over, they handed me the large envelope with the thank-you cards, flower cards, condolence cards, death certificate, and all the other crap that goes with death and burials. I sat and wrote the thank-you cards that evening at Grandma's.

When they closed the casket and I began to cry, Jon escorted me outside. He held me while I cried those tears of the eldest granddaughter who had just lost her grandpa, a grandpa who never said no to her and was always willing to sit and listen to her stories. His hands were enormous and always had extra quarters for us grandkids so we could go to the store to buy candy, and he always laughed at our corny jokes. He could till a garden faster than anyone I had ever seen, too.

It would be decades before I learned the truth about this man. Thinking back now, it is best that I didn't know then what I know now. I would be a different person without a doubt. This is one of the reasons I question organized religion, especially Heaven and Hell. If this man, after all that he has done in his life, can, on his last day, "repent" and be welcomed into Heaven . . . then there is no God. How can you leave those he ruined in this life to torture themselves for his cruelty, his bastardization upon this earth, and then, as if nothing happened . . . okay, come on in! Let's have a beer! What the fuck ever!

Fuck that motherfucking bullshit. We live it every day! Every fucking day! Heaven or Hell—you choose each day when you wake up.

August and September of 1996 were also filled with drama, trauma, and, as if an attempt by the universe to bring balance, also some beauty. My beautiful niece was born in August of 1996. I married my love in September of 1996. And while on our honeymoon, one of my favorite cousins and her youngest son were killed in a car accident about two blocks from my grandmother's home. Paula left behind two toddlers, now without a mother, and she died just ten days past her twenty-fifth birthday and on my twenty-seventh birthday.

We found out my sister was pregnant during that Thanksgiving visit just before Grandpa died. She had been told she could not have children, so she stopped taking birth control. She smoked and drank throughout her entire pregnancy. We worried about how this child was going to survive the lifestyle my sister had chosen during her pregnancy. Thankfully, she presented as a healthy, beautiful—although tiny—human. She is amazing, especially given the gene pool she had to work with and the trauma she endured while trying to become a tiny human.

My wedding was less than a month away. Grandma quickly sewed this tiny princess a dress to match the wedding party. The dress and she were both so tiny, so perfect, and so beautiful.

The wedding was beautiful. The weather was perfect. The family and friends were perfect. We took everyone on a two-story yacht and a three-hour tour at sunset for the reception. The pictures captured the happiness, goofiness, and pure joy of our union. They also would be some of the last pictures of my brother, especially all dressed up.

Paula was extra special to me, as she was one of the ones whom I had told about the bad uncle. When we were younger, Grandma would put Paula, me, and my sister all in the same bed in the front bedroom. Always under at least three quilts—even in the sweltering Mississippi summertime.

The three of us would giggle for hours until Grandma would come in and scold us. We would giggle for a bit more until Grandpa came in and really told us to go to sleep. She, too, was a bold soul, like my uncle and my brother. Fearless, but also shy. As in, she would try anything with enthusiasm, but if you tried to take her picture, she was shy and bashful. She was also a very good cook. After our grandfather's funeral, the cousins all met at her house. We ate and drank, talked and laughed, and even took a few pictures. It was healing and full of love for us all. She was an amazing human and is dearly missed.

In January of 1997, my father's mother died. No need to go to that funeral, though. She still hated us. Funerals are for paying your last respects. There was no respect in either direction.

My brother's death in October of 1998 finally brought an end to the whirlpool of death, and family death chaos. The real chaos for me, though, was just beginning.

By then, I had also filed and had been granted a divorce. I considered bowing out of this life yet again. Sometimes it is just too much, and there is no visible way out. Maybe that's how my brother felt, too, the night he took his life.

The next few years were filled with a darkness I couldn't seem to escape. A depression I hid as best I could from everyone around me. I struggled to work, I struggled to keep in touch with friends or family, and I really just wanted to die inside my dark apartment, knowing the demons surrounded me in every corner. The darkness seemed my only friend and secret confidant. All those who were meant to protect me were now tainted with lies, selfishness, and betrayal and could never be trusted again. How fucking sad was I now, and who would even want to be anywhere near this shit show of my life?

I was divorced, broken, sad, angry, and struggling not to lash out in a rage-filled murderous rampage. Those fuckers deserved it! Maybe I could just become some obscure vigilante sniper taking out all of the child molesters, no-good fathers and mothers, and all-around useless motherfuckers. Maybe that's my real life's calling. I had no doubt I would be the best of the best in that field; my struggle was surviving once I made the most-wanted lists. If I could have figured that out with my limited twenty-eight years of life, this would be a very different story.

I felt unloved, unworthy, and unclean. I didn't want anyone or anything to be exposed to my filth for fear of tainting the fabric of their lives, too. I would endure this pain and suffering alone in an effort to save all others from it. Although, in truth, we all know how my saving someone turned out. How can someone like me be worthy of living if my sweet, fearless brother didn't deserve to live? Or Uncle Billy or sweet Paula?

I should have been there for them. I should have done things differently.

I knew for sure I didn't deserve to be alive, especially after the way I had treated my brother—with all of the tough love, Al-Anon indoctrination, and all-around blinders avoiding the truth of his situation. How could I have been so arrogant as to believe I deserved or would ever achieve anything meaningful in this life? My *one job* was to protect my brother and sister. *Clearly, I'll fail at this life*, I thought. *Look what I've done to theirs.*

I was struggling to even pretend that control was an option. Tightening the loose boards on this sinking ship. Adding expensive attire to be seen as the well-preserved yet hollowed-out human I'd become. Just add it to the list of "holy shit, what the fuck just happened" of my entire life. Smile, hold your head up, and keep walking.

In truth, I was hoping to be swallowed up by life and fade into an abyss so deep they would never find me. There, no one would know what I had done. I had allowed my own desires, my own pain, to deter me from protecting my little brother. Now he was dead, and it was my fault.

I was barely functioning, but I guess we were all just trying to survive then. I was twenty-nine, my sister was twenty-seven, and my brother was now deceased.

Christmas of 1998 sucked.

Madness In The Bloodline

♥

There are books, quotes, and memes about how your sister is your first true friend. If those are true, it would be a testament to my hesitancy toward friendship.

My memories of us before age seven are not so bad. She and I are one year and eleven months apart to the day. We have all heard the story about how I was a mistake, an accident in the backseat, and the reason my parents were together at all.

But my sister—she became a competition for my mom and *her* sister. Aunt Linda was pregnant with my cousin Paula— yes, that cousin Paula—and my mom was pregnant with my sister. They had a sort of contest to see who was going to give birth first.

As it turned out, my sister was born first. Most likely from trauma-induced labor . . . trauma from dear old dad. My sister was born on August 17, my cousin Paula, on September 7. My mom and my aunt Linda still laugh and talk about that rivalry to this day.

My sister showed up as a skeptic. She didn't trust anyone except Mom, which created their special bond out of the gate. During all of those lessons in the backyard with dear old dad about guns, bow and arrows, knives, cars, etc. . . . my sister was clutching her baby doll in the kitchen, following Mom's every move. This gave our dad fodder with which to torture my sister at every turn, which caused Mom to be even more protective of her. It also fueled talk that my sister would be pregnant by age fifteen and probably have a house full of kids.

There was a time when my sister was cute, funny, and fun to be around. Her cheeks were the fattest cheeks in all the land when we were kids. Paula, Shad, my brother, my sister, and I would sit around for hours, laughing at my sister's antics with her cheeks. She could take a rubber band and wrap it around both cheeks, under her chin, and still talk. Sort of like today's Tom the cat animation stuff, but this was real life. It was hilarious! We would literally roll on the floor laughing at those antics back then.

As we got older, it was evident she could not be trusted. If the five of us snuck out and walked to the store, she would tattle on us as soon as Mom got home. Even if she was in on it, and even if it was her idea!

She was also not a very neat or tidy person, either. Mom, however, always wanted everything clean and presentable. My sister would shove her toys, clothes, whatever under my bed or on my side of the closet when it was time to clean. Mom would come in, and I would get into trouble even though I legitimately cleaned my things. Mom wouldn't hear my argument for one second. My sister was standing there silent, clutching her baby doll, acting innocent. I guess that's how most siblings are, right?

When we were really, really young, Mom would dress her and me as twins, sewing the same outfit for both of us and dressing us in the same outfit on the same day. In hindsight, it was probably easier for Mom to remember who wore what on which day, but it was truly humiliating for me. (As I flip my hair back, saying, I'm the oldest, after all.)

There was no skipping school, either, if my sister knew about it. Mom would know about it before it even happened.

It was during this time that I learned the hard lesson that if you're going to be an adult, you cannot be ashamed of your decisions. Own it and go with it. If you are not doing anything wrong, then there is no reason to hide it. Right? Except I wasn't quite an adult yet. But hey, they were treating me like one, so . . . here I am! This was, and is, a resounding theme throughout my life.

I remember when I told my sister and Paula about the bad uncle. They both gasped and told me that was not okay, but my sister is the one who got up early and told the adults the next day. Before Paula and I were even awake, trouble was brewing. Oh, the tangled web we weave.

I never told her about our dad and that day when he pulled me out of the pool. I know now that this is why. She would have told, and it wouldn't have been in a planned, chess-move kind of telling. More of a blurting-it-out way. Like throwing the gauntlet into the arena and seeing who comes out. Yes! That was always her style. It makes so much more sense now as I write this. Lashing out, throwing spears into the air, and seeing if anyone survives. That's how she does everything in her life, it would seem now.

When we were old enough to drive, Mom gifted us each a car. Mine was a '78 Mustang (another bluebird). She was a four-cylinder, T-tops, hatchback. The radio didn't work, the hatchback wouldn't stay up, and the T-tops leaked . . . but I loved her. My sister rode with me on my paper route after school. One day, as we were heading to pick up our papers, an old lady T-boned us at an intersection. The T-tops were off, and my sister literally flew out of her side and into my lap. Seatbelts were optional, always. That lady was pissed off when she plowed into us. She was leaving a seedy motel, so my guess was the sex was bad, or he had just broken up with her for a younger model. Either way, she chose to take it out on us teeny-boppers.

Thankfully, no one was seriously injured, and the afternoon papers were delivered on time. But my car was nearly totaled.

About three months before graduation in my senior year, my sister drove my car to follow my mom to drop her car off for service. My sister was swiped by another vehicle during that drive, and the insurance company totaled my car. I was furious. My mother and sister were oblivious to my pain; after all, it wasn't them or their transportation at the precipice of their moment of freedom. After my sister totaled my car, Mom bought my sister a car—a VW bug—also bluebird blue.

Mom told me that I could use whatever money I had saved from working my two jobs, and she would give me $1,000 toward graduation that I could spend on my next vehicle. Mind you, my sister did not work any jobs. She merely "helped" me on my paper route, which I was solely responsible for with my mother and with the Sun Herald.

The level of betrayal I felt at that time would haunt all other dealings with my mother for the rest of my life. And especially if it also involved my sister or money in any way. I also knew, at that moment, my mother would never be on my side. She would make sure that I learned some lesson from any financial dealings that involved her. A lesson I would never have wanted to believe but was the truth, as evident throughout any dealings with my mother.

My sister was never required to work for Mom to bend over backward, making sure my sister's life was not in any way a discomfort. The sages and wisdom speakers would later tell me this is because I am the "stronger" one and that my mother knew my sister needed more help in this life. Bunch of fucking bullshit. *Whatever, I got this.* Spoken like a true, broken-hearted teenage badass who was left with no other option.

Just before my favorite uncle died, Mom had had a dream that someone was murdered. Someone in our family. Part of her psychic ability that she refused to acknowledge . . . or, maybe she wasn't allowed to, either.

As Mother's Day approached, we made plans to meet at Mom's that morning for brunch. I was, as usual, on time. My sister, however, didn't answer her phone for several hours and finally showed up about three hours later. Mom continued to rake the leaves in her front yard the whole time. As my sister and I began arguing about what a disrespectful piece of shit she was for not showing up on time, not even calling to say she would be late . . . Mom became more and more agitated and only then told us of her dream. I left. *What the fuck ever. This is some bullshit.* It is always about my sister, and only she matters. If my mom had thought for one second that I was the one who was going to die, I have no doubt her world would have been okay. But since she assumed it would be my sister who died—or had died, according to her dream—now we have a different situation. So Mom wanted to keep me close until she knew for sure. Fuck any other plans I had for that day or that I was self-employed and needed to prepare for the week ahead!

Nope, always about Kim.

"Kim needs me more than you," she would say. "You are doing all right on your own." This was my mother's answer. Really? And how do you not see the correlation between you and I and Kim and your sister? Again, really?

Holy fucking shit. What did I just step into, and how do I get the fuck out of it?

Worse yet, you know how hard you had to work for what you have. How can you not see that maybe I am the one who actually needs help if we, as a family, are ever going to get out of this shit show! WTF!

Fine, I got this one, too. Nah, don't worry. I am strong, remember?

I got this—this passive-aggressive behavior—also a learned trait from those days.

Anger, bitterness, resentment. Not something I expected when writing this chapter. Toward my sister, yes, of course. But not toward my mother. Although my sister will tell you straight up that all of her issues are my mother's fault. Which to me seems ironic—but whatever. What do I fucking know?

My sister gave birth to a beautiful baby girl after a particularly traumatic evening with my brother. We all waited and slept crankily and uncomfortably in that hospital waiting room. From the moment she showed up, the only voice she really responded to was my mother's voice. That's how she got the nickname Turtle. The nurse brought her into the room, placed her in my sister's arms, and then my mother spoke. That sweet, beautiful child raised her head and looked in the direction of my mother's voice. We all gasped and then laughed, and then she was called Turtle. As if she was sticking her head out of her shell to the sound of freedom and safety.

Giving birth to that amazing little girl is, in my opinion, the only redeeming quality my sister has or ever will have. Sounds harsh. I know. But then, the truth is sometimes harsh. There are just some people who are bad humans, and this could be a family trait—my father and my sister.

During the trials and situations with my brother, she mostly stayed away. Although she will most likely tell you that she was there every step of the way unless she thinks you will show more sympathy if she says she was "just too scared and heartbroken" to be there through it all. The psychopathic tendencies were evident long before I even knew what that word meant. Thankfully, there is a term for that.

There are a number of psychology books dealing with situations such as ours. Including one about children growing up in the same household and becoming very different adults . . . as in, how did this happen? We all grew up in the same household, and our mother was there with us through it all. Yet each of us sees the events of our horrific past differently. So differently, in fact, that my sister will most likely tell you we had a great childhood.

There is no doubt in my mind that my sister believes her delusions, at least in the moment. Someone always seems to be chasing her, someone coming after her or her daughter— to collect on past debts. One night, she started sending text messages to my mom and me about being in a speeding car. She said she wasn't driving but was certain someone had drugged her at the last bar. She told us who she "thought" she was with but didn't know where they were going or where they had been or how she got there. We kept pushing her for more information, and thankfully, her young daughter was with my mom and me on that night. My sister signed off for the night by saying something to the effect of she is safe now and knows where she is. She never would tell us where that was.

The first dozen or so times this happened, Mom and I would actually go look for her and be worried. After that, it was just a normal day for my sister wanting chaos to ensue and making everything all about her. Forget that she had a young daughter she was supposed to be a "mother" to. Nope, all about Kim and fuck everyone else. So you're stressed out and worried for her safety after a text like that? So fucking what?! She is fine, and the next day she'll act as though nothing happened, and that you are making everything up. Even when you show her the fucking text messages. It was, *Someone else must have sent those, I didn't send those.*

Pathological.

The past decade has been super peaceful without the extra drama from her, and I cannot help but wonder if she, too, isn't schizophrenic. At a minimum, she is and always has been mentally unstable.

As adults, there were a number of times my sister and I attempted to have a relationship. However, when we would try to "talk about the old days," our stories were very different, right down to the people who were present, what each one did, and details like that. It was frightening to hear her version of some events. For instance, there was one time, driving home in the rain with my sister and Trena in the car with me. My tires were not the best, and they were also low-profile tires—I mean, I still had to be sort of cool. This wasn't just any rain. This was a torrential downpour resulting in small rivers in the streets. We slid in a curve and into an embankment. I was able to pull back out onto the road and get us home. However, the sliding and mud resulted in two flat tires on the passenger side of my little S10 truck. Well, not totally flat, I suppose. They were filled with mud.

In my sister's version of this story, the truck flipped over two or three times, and then I drove us home.

The embellishments continued to the point that I just had to straight out call her a liar to her face. I was the one fucking driving! I know what happened. And if we would have rolled at all, we would all be dead. That truck would have never protected us.

 Her need for attention, her need for drama-filled, trauma-inducing chaos, is at times overwhelming. She is truly a selfish human being and was quite upset that I was the one molested because it took the attention off of her. She said I just wanted to take all of the attention. Are you fucking kidding me right now? Exactly. This is the type of psychopath we have on our hands.

Therapists and elders alike would say she was "just jealous" of me and that I should go easier on her and take it as a compliment. Again, are you fucking kidding me right now? She causes total chaos in my life, and nothing I have ever done has ever been good enough for her or my mother.

Finally, a therapist told me what I wanted to hear. He told me that just because she is "blood kin" doesn't mean I have to necessarily have her in my day-to-day life. I can "love her from afar."

I cut my sister out of my life when she took her husband's side (not my niece's father) over her own daughter. And then tried to blame my mom for all of it. It has been over a decade since I have seen or spoken to my sister. I do not feel I have lost anything, and for the most part, my life has been blissfully peaceful.

Making Peace
with mom.

No matter how many therapists you see, state lines you run screaming across, healing modalities or medications you try—no matter the length of the rivers of your tears flooding every small town east of the Mississippi—it will never ease the perceived betrayal of your own mother.

We are trained from a very young age, and especially once we enter school, that our mothers are "supposed" to be our fiercest protector and provider.

For me, growing up feeling that I needed to somehow protect my mom and my siblings as best as I could as a child were the only words ringing in my ears during my adolescence. *Don't do anything to embarrass your momma, and don't do anything that may get her murdered by your father.*

There is no consoling a child who feels abandoned and unprotected by their mother and/or father. This is an especially brutal conviction in the South. If your own mother doesn't want you or love you, no one else should or will, either.

How can you possibly escape that entrenched into your bloodline belief?

Especially when the betrayal, the abandonment, the indifference are all still so raw. They are still oozing with self-disdain, self-loathing, and self-hate. There is nothing a therapist can say or do that will apply enough salve to allow these wounds to cauterize and begin to heal. No. There is nothing the outside world can do to release you from that prison. That lock must be picked from within, and by no one else but yourself.

Super cliché, but there's also super truth in that statement. The amount of self-loathing, self-flagellation, is not even apparent during most of that journey.

When we begin to allow our adult parents to be just human, not our parents, when we begin to see them as just another person who crossed our path, we somehow begin to "let them off the hook" for so much. My dear friend, Cinimon, has repeated this statement to me for many decades. She would tell me to let my mother off the hook so that both my mother and I could find some fucking peace. I wasn't ready then. I was still angry, still oh-so-very angry. Angry at her for not protecting herself. Or me. Or us. Angry at her for staying with that sorry motherfucker all of those years. Angry at her for telling me all about the trouble we were in but not allowing me to be part of the team to get us out. Angry at her for never really wanting my help, seemingly—only my sympathy or empathy. Angry that she could not see any greatness within me, much less any good.

I'll show her how good I am. I will show her what a badass I can be, and am. You just hide and watch.

Maybe that was her goal after all, to push me to push myself. To love myself.

This . . . this is where my fight started for survival, for validation, for . . . love. The barriers and walls went up, and I compartmentalized every fucking thing down to the tiniest detail. If it wasn't part of my path to prove myself, it wasn't part of my life. Every time someone told me I wasn't enough, or that I couldn't do this or that, they might as well have tossed a lit match on those swaying pine trees lined with overgrowth and lighter knot, soaked in fucking diesel fuel. Diesel fuel so the trail doesn't lead back to me. *Fuck those motherfuckers. I'll show them!*

At least, that was me in my late teens and early twenties. If I'm being honest, probably just over the threshold of my thirties, too.

I worked extra hard and made life hard on myself and everyone around me during those years. *Too bad if you're tired. Too bad if you can't sleep. Get to work and quit your whining. That money ain't gonna make itself.*

When it came to working, I was never afraid of hard work. Most of my life I have had at least two jobs at all times with the constant being the insurance industry.

Before I moved to Idaho, I don't ever recall my mother telling me she was proud of me—*ever*. The first time wasn't until I accepted a position making substantially more than anyone else in my family, at least as far as we knew.

I didn't quite understand it then, but nonetheless, it shifted something within me. I would be doing the same job I had always been doing, only now it would be on someone else's schedule and timing. But now? *Now?* She was proud of me. Was it always about the money? Nah, couldn't have been. I made a ton tending bar in Atlanta while I built up my insurance business.

My psychological demons started playing tricks on me then. Was she proud of me because I had convinced someone else to want me? Someone else to pay me a lot of money? Did she somehow feel I had betrayed these people, and that's why they were paying me, and that's why she was proud of me? For being a smooth talker? Or was she proud of me then because she never thought I could do it? And when I did, she felt obligated to tell me she was proud of me?

It took me a few months to talk myself down from these thoughts. I kept hearing her voice over and over in my head, her words, that day. Telling me she was proud of me. Her words didn't sound forced or coerced. They sounded genuine. Again, my friend reminded me to cut my mom some fucking slack.

As trauma survivors, we have this innate ability to be the chameleon we need to be, to be accepted into nearly any situation. The challenges don't show up until you have to believe in yourself, and no one else's faith in you is enough.

When the only person that really needs to bet on you—bet on your success—is yourself, that's when you realize just how much hatred and self-loathing you've been carrying.

My friends and I discuss parenthood openly now. Not that I am a parent, necessarily, but I can see a larger picture: a high, aerial view of the situation at hand.

When we were in Atlanta, to relieve some of the stress of the situation with my brother, my mom and I would go out dancing. She didn't learn until much later that I actually had a fake ID that said I was twenty-one. Most of the places in Atlanta, at that time, allowed you to enter at eighteen. What Mom didn't know was that they would put one of those bracelets on you that let everyone know you weren't twenty-one yet—especially the bartenders.

We had such a good time, though! There was this bar called T-Birds where they had all of these cool, old cars inside and outside of the bar. They played all kinds of music but mostly the old school stuff that was fucking fabulous and easy to dance to. There was also a place off of Jimmy Carter Boulevard—or JCB, if you were part of the cool crowd. Can't remember the name of that place, and it changed names about every two years or so.

Mom had a friend who taught country dance lessons there. Sometimes, she would wear country and western outfits. She was like a supermodel for country line dancing. It was fantastic. I could walk into the place and instantly, everyone knew exactly who my mother was and who I was. If memory serves, we held her fortieth birthday party there.

I find some level of irony in the fact that my mom and I both spent our fortieth birthdays in Atlanta. Two small town Mississippi gals living it up in the big city.

From there, it gets a little wonky, though.

The thought of my mom moving three kids to the big city of Atlanta . . . knowing *one* person in the whole fucking state! Maybe that's where my adventurous side came from? The whole, "I'm gonna do it anyway!" attitude makes perfect sense now, right? All the more reason moving to Idaho didn't seem like such a big deal to me. Maybe she was preparing me for my future without even realizing it.

There have probably been times in your life when someone or lots of someones have told you how great you are at XYZ, or what a great person you are, or that you should try ABC because you'd be really good at it. All of these others seem to be able to see our greatness, but we are blinded by its very beauty, like a butterfly unable to see its own wings. No matter how many people believe in us, telling us how great we are—how pretty, how attractive, how smart, how fill in the fucking blank—we are never going to truly believe it.

Nope, that belief in yourself must be rebuilt from the inside, like a waterlogged carburetor from a tanker truck drowned at the bottom of the pond after the last hurricane.

Someone must dive down there, remove all of the wires and extended cables, retrieve the carburetor, and return to the surface. Then, it must be removed from the hard shell casing, each tiny piece completely dismantled, washed clean, allowed to dry, and then reassembled with new grease, oil, and sometimes new parts or pieces.

Eh, the dismantling seems easy enough, right? Especially when we *think* we can control the dismantling. We all know it needs to be done, so just make that shit happen!

Okay, I am dismantled. Now what?

Then, some part of that carburetor is needed in our lives, and we rush the necessary pieces back together and ride along, listening to the clunking and coughing, watching the smoke billowing from underneath, knowing we did a shoddy job. Knowing we slapped it all back together in a heated rush to move on. To move on and away from that trauma, from that old movie playing in our head.

We continue to smoke and rattle along until the next major emotional event forces us to dismantle once again. We may even scrub those same pieces a little better this time; that must be it! We just didn't clean *those* pieces enough. Pretending all of the other parts are irrelevant. After all, we just rolled down the road with just these cleaned up. It's fine; everything will be just fine.

That's what we tell ourselves to avoid the really dirty parts that need cleaning. You know, the ones with the old grease caked on so thick it looks like someone had a Mississippi mud pie party in there. Some parts are all gritty and slimy, too. Nah, a quick wipe on those. We're all good here. Does any of this sound familiar?

Yup, I thought so.

No one tells us how long this process will take or how long that carburetor will be soaking in the tub before those parts get really good and clean. That's where perseverance comes into play: continuing to work on ourselves, continuing to clean out all of the yucky parts, and also being gentle so as not to break any pieces or damage them further. Continuing to grow into the best version of ourselves that we can possibly be. And sometimes, it is about forgiveness. Forgiveness of ourselves, mostly. Because in all truthfulness, the person we are most upset with is ourselves.

Forgiving ourselves for abandoning our younger selves in favor of survival mode—"handle it" mode. Forgiveness of ourselves for not knowing how to protect our younger selves from predators. Forgiveness of ourselves for holding the anger, the hurt, the fear, and the sadness for so long. Forgiveness of ourselves for continuing to try to win over those who dismissed us.

Forgiveness of ourselves for continuing to try to win the approval of those who will never give it . . . maybe not out of spite or vengeance, but because they just don't know how. They were never taught, and no one ever approved of them either.

In our society, the assumption is that women just show up in this world knowing how to be mothers. Women must instinctively know how to raise children, buy groceries for a great meal, cook a good meal, please their man sexually, heal the sick, raise the downtrodden. You get the idea. Sort of makes sense. After all, women were historically considered to be witches. I mean, can a man bleed for three to seven days and not die? Can a man take a tiny sperm and turn it into a human being in less than a year? These last two are things that nature just steps in and helps a woman handle. The rest also depends on how she was raised, her surroundings, the people around her—and especially the women she was surrounded with as a young girl.

It also matters what she was taught about raising children, cooking meals, healing the sick, and what others did when she was the child, when it was she who was sick. Did they teach her that she mattered? That her thoughts, feelings, dreams, and goals mattered? Or was she brushed aside, leaving her trauma unhealed, unacknowledged, and avoided at all costs?

This is another place where things get a little sideways. As the oldest child, even though I was a girl, I was taught to "take care of" the women. If there wasn't a man around, it was my job to be the "man." Sometimes, even if there was a man around, and he wasn't doing his job, I was told to step in and . . . you guessed it . . . handle it. I had to open doors, carry the heavy things, do the man chores, etc. During my early childhood, I saw this as an opportunity to prove my worth, my value in this world. My desire to please and be worthy superseded all else during those years.

As these habits carried into adulthood, it was viewed more as a sexuality preference. Especially after moving to the big city of Atlanta. Being from podunk Mississippi, I was ill-prepared for this. To me, I was just being the dutiful daughter; to the outside world, I was "trying to be a man" by taking care of the women around me.

This also gets confusing because in my adult life, I am and always have been a fierce and aggressive protector of women. In Atlanta, there was many a time when I would step in between a man hitting a woman in the bars or on the streets. This usually ended up with the males nearby feeling threatened and then also coming quickly to the scene.

Which leads to another confusing behavior of mine. Competition with males.

Competition, in general, isn't necessarily a bad thing. But when you are a five-foot-nothing tiny woman challenging a man's ego . . . now, we have some shit going down.

Ironically, this got me into some really hot water in Atlanta. Let's just say that my aggressive, assertive behavior led to a group of gay men—who became some of my best friends during my time there—teaching me how to "properly" give a blow job. But that's a story for another time.

Guess this goes right along with the construction in Atlanta. It always seems to be going on, nonstop. Kind of like our own personal growth and learning—always under construction.

Throughout history, women are also taught that women must compete with each other. Competition for the best mate, competition for the best job, the best life. We have been taught to ridicule, judge, even punish other women should they attempt to move ahead in life. Thankfully, this is starting to turn around. Perhaps back then, they feared us, as women all working together, supporting each other, helping each other. That makes the most logical sense for these teachings. A group of women working toward a common goal, now that's a beautiful sight to behold. The world needs more of that.

There is currently very little in this world that tells you how to heal and how long it takes to heal, and nothing that tells us how broken we will feel after being dismantled and trying to piece it all back together. There is no manual about how to handle life except by example of those around us. Which isn't always the greatest or easiest way to get through this thing called life.

Especially when you come from podunk Mississippi. Any attempts to escape that, and you will be branded a traitor— someone who thinks they are better than everyone else. You will be labeled a troublemaker; a ne'er-do-well who thinks her shit don't stink. This is where you sort of learn to pick your battles. Survival? Or exposure? You think they mock you now while you're trying to do better for yourself? Wait until you expose the dark secrets they told you not to tell!

Exposing those secrets is the very thing that shifted my relationship with my mother. As a young girl, as a teenager, as a young adult, I only saw her one way: as my mother. I never asked why she was that way, and she never told. And, I never told her I was proud of her.

Until that day.

Into The
Gator's Mouth

*T*herapy is a funny thing. Sometimes you have to visit a few therapists to find one who feels right to you. For me, it had to be someone who would not allow me to deflect so easily and change the subject—someone who would also be brave enough to call me on my own shit. I found that therapist right before my brother's death, thankfully. Perhaps the gods were looking out for me.

He was Jewish, straightforward, and pulled no punches with me. He reminded me that we are all human and that we are all going through our own storms. Viewing those storms through our own filter, our own warped reality because of what we have seen, heard, and been through already.

He also reminded me that my mother was human with her own childhood story, one I knew nothing about. Sure, we heard stories about her life growing up—picking cotton, picking green beans, sewing her long skirt up on the school bus to be a cool mini-skirt-wearing hipster. But there were others we never knew anything about.

There is also the difference between a parent and a grandparent. As grandparents, much like being the cool aunt, you really only have to do the fun stuff. It is up to the parents to do the majority of the disciplining, the homework, the baths, and that bedtime routine that sometimes results in meltdowns. As a grandparent, you get to laugh and have fun with the children. You can spoil them in ways that you probably couldn't afford to do when your own children were growing up. In those children's eyes, that grandparent is a special and dear person with amazing powers of laughter and fun. They are not the person that raised your mom or dad. Nope, they've turned into a whole different human now. At least in the eyes of that grandchild.

This grandparent adventure is great except that it affords us a make-believe life that allows us to forget this is the same person who raised our mom or dad. As our parents scold us or swat us on our backside to get us back in line, we forget they learned this from their parents. Yep! Those same sweet grandparents who can do no wrong in our six-year-old eyes as they spoil us with goodies and special trips and gifts. Our parents don't forget, though. As a child, it is hard to believe that would ever be the case. Our grandparents would never be so mean as to scold or swat a child!

In our world today, the behavior of the grandparents while raising their children is exactly what the new parents are fighting against when they refuse to do things the same way. This is how we ended up with "time-out" rather than a good swat on the behind. This is how we ended up with regulated or sometimes unregulated bedtimes for toddlers: bucking the system. Healthier foods, different clothes, shoes, electronics or no electronics . . . the list can go on for decades. My point is, we learned what to do and also what not to do from our parents and the other adults we were surrounded with as children. Psychologists would refer to this as our environment.

Some, such as myself, choose to buck the system completely by not having children of our own. Take that, Freud!

As adults, it is our opportunity to take a step back and look at our parents' lives differently. From the perspective of an outsider, really. Otherwise, our emotions cloud our perception, our reasoning, and our judgment. I am not saying carte blanche forgiveness is appropriate in all situations. And in some cases, there is no amount of reasoning or perception that makes a parent's behavior okay. Sometimes, there are just bad humans in the world, and that is not your fault either. And besides, this forgiveness is just for you. It is not about them. They have to do their own growth work. This is about you and your healing; your freedom lies on the other side of forgiving yourself.

Fuck those motherfuckers.

When I decided this book must be written and the truth (my truth) must be told, I was admonished to tell my mother about the book prior to its publication. People gave me scenarios about how cruel it would be to just drop the finished product in her lap and say, "Here you go. Here's your copy of my trauma for your records." That sounded pretty shitty, and I consider myself a good human. So talk to my mother it was, before I got too far into this drowning pool.

I will be honest. It was a struggle to summon the courage to tell her about it. I hadn't even told her about my blog! I played the dialogue in my head over and over, changing pieces, changing my tone, changing seating positions. I meditated and asked my guides for help. My stomach was in knots, and I was really wound up about it—all of it. My relationship with my mother already wasn't the easiest. In fact, "strained" would probably be the most accurate description. The funny thing was, there was no particular reason for it to be so strained. We're just two different people who happen to be mother and daughter . . . at least that's what I told myself as I prepared for my conversation with her.

After a few weeks of making myself physically ill, I decided just to text her one Saturday morning. Yes, I know, it would seem I could just call her, but then I wouldn't know what kind of mood she was in. No need to stick my head in the gator's mouth unnecessarily. She responded quickly and said she was home, alone, cleaning, and seemed to be in pretty good spirits. So I called her.

After catching up on all of the small-town gossip and family matters, I told her I was writing a book. I told her that I needed her to know that she is not the villain in this book. I told her that, in actuality, she had to be one badass motherfucker for any of us to have survived at all. She was silent for a moment and then told me that the best thing to do was just to let that stuff go. It's in the past, and there's nothing you can do about it now. I told her I had tried that route, and it isn't working for me. People—damaged people—seek me out in the oddest of places and tell me their story, as if we have been lifelong friends. They seem finally unburdened and able to move on by telling me their stories. Usually, they even hug me and thank me. For what? For being a damaged soul, for being a damaged soul who they could share their truth with, without judgment. I have to tell my story, Mom.

We didn't talk about it after that, but as luck would have it, they were planning to come here to Idaho for Christmas. You know, one of them there white Christmases they sing about.

My mom and stepdad arrived first, nearly a full week ahead of my niece and her husband. I was extremely nervous about how this was going to go since it would be the first time we had seen each other since I told her about the book. She hadn't asked to read it. She didn't ask where she could find my blogs. She didn't ask anything about it at all, which was a relief and also another dagger all at the same time. Didn't she care? Of course she did. She simply needed a moment to process what I had said.

One evening after dinner, as we sat in the living room just visiting and talking, she broke the ice. We stayed up well past 2 a.m. talking about my father, the abuse, the bad uncle, even some about my brother. No one cried, but the softness in the air felt like a blanket warmed by the sun holding me tightly.

There were a few pieces of our stories that didn't match our separate and individual memories. We acknowledged the discrepancy and kept moving toward healing discussions. She went to bed first, with my stepdad and I staying up to mull over what had been said, some of which, he confessed, he had heard for the first time just this evening. It felt as if the six blankets deeply smothering me had finally been moved enough to allow air to flow through.

When she got up the next morning, she told me she remembered some of the things I had said that happened that she hadn't remembered the night before. The whole visit was one of our best ones yet. We had at least one other evening of these talks, and it seemed that a huge shift occurred between us. At least for me. Finally, some salve for the unhealed gashes left over from a childhood none could move past.

It was also strange for me as an adult woman to see my mother as a human being with feelings of her own. While she and I and my brother and my sister were all in those moments together, we were all also in our own heads, hearts, and minds. Those experiences are jaded by whatever else was also going on in our lives in those moments. How could I possibly know what it was like for her to go through those times as a wife, as a mother, as a daughter? All clouded over with her own cement-block-weighted-down suitcase of trauma that she was already drowning in. *And* dragging three kids.

For the first time, I could see the hurt—visibly see the hurt my mother felt describing her feelings and emotions during those times. Not that I didn't think she felt anything before, but until now, I couldn't allow her to just be a human being rather than the mom that left me standing there without guidance. She didn't have any to give because no one gave her any either. She did the best she knew how and she made it out of that podunk place and has made an incredible life for herself.

I think the healing can begin in the allowing another person to be human and feel what they feel without judgment or expectation. Sometimes, we get caught up in our own heads, in our own trauma or ideals of how this should be or that should be. We forget that that other person also has their ideals, their trauma, the way they think it should be. It would seem that the very definition of unconditional love is somewhere in the middle of allowing others to feel what they feel, be who they are without comparison, without condemnation, but with compassion in this new beautiful space of acceptance.

Danger In The Damage

♥

*D*amaged people are not people to be fucked with. They have survived more than most will ever experience in this lifetime. Damaged people always seem to be walking that invisible edge that only other damaged people can see. That edge is really more like a light switch—stop or go—with no in between.

In my early twenties I took up Ninjutsu as a way to expel and also learn to control my anger and rage. I was barely one hundred pounds soaking wet, but I was *very* angry. Martial arts, in general, are not for the faint of heart. You will walk away with bruises and sometimes broken bones. Unless you are holding back and not participating fully, which our Sensei would never tolerate. He was a retired police officer and about my height.

One day, during a sparring session, I was paired up with a six-foot biker dude. I knew this was going to hurt and I was looking forward to every minute of it.

Our Sensei came over to me during one of the take-down moves and said, "That was good, but you still look afraid. Imagine all one hundred pounds of your weight on his windpipe. Do you think he will get back up then?"

He then proceeded to show me several moves for people our height (read: short people) to use in situations just like this one. Thankfully, my biker partner was agreeable to allowing me to practice on him, and I was ultimately able to put him on his back with a thud. I only stayed in this practice for a few years, having moved through some of my fears and anxiety, and also some of my anger. This was the first time I was exposed to meditation, although I didn't know that was what we were doing.

Since then, I have also taken several gun courses and learned to shoot straight and with a steady hand, leaving behind all that my dear old dad had taught me. All in favor of learning at my own pace, in my own way, and from someone I actually trusted to teach me correctly and properly. Not under any duress. No yelling, no back-handed slaps. Only growth and learning in a wide open space that was just mine.

In the movies, we have all seen how the most vicious, trainable killer is the one with nothing to lose. Typically, they have no immediate family: parents died in a car accident, never married, no children, etc. Damaged people can be like that, too. They may still have close family, but they also feel the brevity of being alone and on their own with no one but themselves coming to "save" them.

How many people do we walk past every day, never realizing what they may have been through in this life? How many of them are on that edge, with one finger on that light switch? Walking through every day pretending they are sane, they are whole, rational, making responsible choices and handling life like every other adult around them? With no one ever realizing that person is one light switch flip away from killing a motherfucker who stepped too close to their demons. One day they are a happy-go-lucky stockbroker, and the next, BAM! Arrested for killing some asshole who pushed their buttons on the wrong day. I think there's a reality series out now about this very thing.

Maybe this is exactly how I have survived this life. Most people tell me I have a "mean mug" look more often than not. It isn't intentional, but I suppose it has served as a sort of warning signal. Several movies come to mind when I think about being in this mindset, where you don't know who you are, but you also really have nothing to lose. Three squares and a cot seem like a cakewalk compared to what you've already been through in this life. *Bring it!*

Or maybe my guides and angels have protected me so well, and that is how I have made it this far. Those motherfuckers must be tired; I have never made it easy for anyone to love me.

Damaged people also seem to have trouble in relationships. Speaking from personal experience, I tend to *ass/u/me* everyone I connect with is meant to stay. Worse, I assume they intend to stay regardless of their words, actions, or how slight our connection may be. Part of me figures if they can see through my mean mug and the walls, they already know what they are signing up for, right? Although, that is probably what they are thinking about me given their "hidden" damage, as well.

Somewhere in the trauma of my childhood is a deep, dark voice that tells me I *must* work extra hard to show them I am worth it. That I am worth loving. Worth keeping. Cue the super-attached control freak, watching their every move for variations in the patterns that might suggest they have changed their mind or are about to change their minds. Any indication of such variations means it is time to work extra hard to convince them I am worth them sticking around and seeing this rough patch through to the end. In hindsight, I would have run from my own shit, too. As if studying their every move and second-guessing their directions would make them move toward me rather than away from me. Good luck with *that*.

My relationships have ranged from, *Oh, this could work!* to *What the actual fuck are you thinking right now?* and everywhere in between. Now, it makes more sense. I was also expecting me from these relationships, which is a sad but common mistake. I was expecting someone who is or at least has been working through their own shit; healing their own mind, body, and soul. Healing themselves in an effort not to taint their next relationship in their pursuit of a true partner in this life. Someone who could be trusted with the scars and stories without judgment, someone who could love me as if I were never damaged or broken.

In the end, I was just looking for someone who didn't make my life harder. But can you really call that an actual relationship? I suppose so. But I cannot imagine it would be a good one and would not last very long on any timetable.

Maybe some part of me feels I don't deserve a good relationship, anyway. My brother will never have another opportunity for a good relationship or even a mediocre one. There are only two men on the planet I have shared my dark secrets with, shared the story of the demons who haunt me in this life. Neither of them are by my side today.

Why not? Because my unworthiness follows me each day, visible across my face like a beacon shining, leading other damaged souls on a virtual tour of what-not-to-do-ness of life. Clearly, I am destined to walk solo in my boots and jeans with my beautifully damaged soul, only visible to the ones who have seen it firsthand in their own lives. On the outside, I look perfectly normal. Sane. Even pretty. Like someone who had an easy childhood and an amazing life.

This couldn't be further from my truth. Yes, I am a peaceful, fun-loving hippie without the drugs and no easy life or childhood, and there is very little that is "normal" here. The person I am today is the flawed perfection that is me.

Death In The mirror

♥

In September of 2000, I jumped out of a perfectly good airplane, praying for death.

Making a deal with the devil within that *if* I survived, I would accept the truth that I must live this life no matter how shitty my past has been. More so, I must live this life as a human and find a way to love myself and those who cared for me.

I survived the skydiving adventure. Special thanks to my then ex-husband for going with me. I didn't want him to jump with me, and I know he didn't understand that then. I only wanted me to die, not him, too. I still loved him. I just didn't love myself.

The next few decades were filled with fits and starts, crying, raging, periods of self-destruct mode, sitting-in-the-corner, throwing-shit-at-myself mode, and lots of therapy—the professional kind and the alcohol and drug kind. Even the therapists would tell me that I should be "way more fucked up" than I was after all I had been through. That's an actual quote from one of those therapists in Atlanta!

I got my first tattoo in 2001 in remembrance of my brother. Brighter than the sun and always has my back.

I spent this time in constant reflection and self-loathing. I asked myself, *What did I do wrong? How do I change? What do I need to change? How could I have been a better person? What signs did I miss? How could I have been so naïve? Why would anyone choose life after all of this shit? What the actual fuck is wrong with me? And now that I am not dead, how do I fucking fix it?*

All questions with no clear answers. The questions just led to more and more self-flagellation, more questions, more doubt about whether or not I was a good human who deserved a good life. Or at least not a bad life. Each moment I allowed those thoughts to consume my everyday life sent me down into the spiral of not-enough-ness.

My friends, kind and caring, would tell me to reach out to them during these down times. That they would gladly help me remember who I am, what kind of person I am, and how much I deserve an amazing life. In fact, I tell them to call me when they reach those levels as well. Each of us truly meant for the other to reach out for a friend with whom to walk through those fires.

The truth is, though, that I was too afraid to reach out. The demons that live in my thoughts are too powerful for me to fight in those moments. They tell me lies that my true friends will ridicule me, judge me, and cast me aside into the still smoldering ashes of my never-was-good-enough-ness. Too powerful for me to see past the raging hot flames of not-enough-ness, like solar flares shooting off in all directions. Spilling fiery flames in all directions, and especially any positive direction I was headed toward.

I was too afraid of the possibility of rejection, too afraid of the possibility of judgment—theirs and my own. What if they sent my call to voicemail or ignored my text message?

What if they were busy with their own demons at that moment and couldn't help me slay mine? Sort of like in a battle scene, where you have to kill everything in front of you before you can get to the woman you love, who is fighting alongside you.

This picture in my mind is of the little girl within me fighting alongside the adult version of me. She looks up at me with fear in her eyes, repeating the question, *Are you going to save me this time?* Questioning if I am going to leave her there, huddled up next to the half-dead demons of the past, still growling and hissing. The demons reaching for her, to drag her back down into the abyss, back into the past, never reaching her full potential as an adult.

Or would I take her by the hand this time and lead her to our life together? To our life now, forever fighting side by side, knowing we will never again leave each other in this life?

What if these friends viewed this as me being too dramatic, seeing this problem only through the eyes of the trauma of my past and not looking toward my future? Drama isn't really something I do, but forgetting who I am *is*. There are some moments when I feel so insecure that they take me back to that place of not-enough-ness. Rather than seeking validation of myself by reminding myself of my accomplishments, the unrelenting demons remind me of my failures, my perceived shortcomings, and show me flashes of my childhood and failed relationships. Flashes of where I came from as a reminder that I will never be good enough, that I am not smart enough, that I didn't come from "enough" to even be enough.

How many times have I been labeled a "failure" by myself or others because of the mess I have left behind? I was doing the best I could given my upbringing and others' past decisions, all the while pretending to be an adult myself. So what? So fucking what if it's messy? So what if my life doesn't look like a sweet Southern girl's life "should" look like, or I don't behave how I "should" behave?

I've spent way too much time trying to stay within the lines, trying not to ruffle too many feathers or kick up too much dust. *Be sweet. Don't say anything if it isn't nice. In fact, keep your fucking mouth shut. You're just a fucking girl!*

I spent many of those nights crying, sobbing, on the floor. I got rug burns from the sobbing and bruises from the tile in the bathroom, throwing up the poison rejected by my liver.

Lots of memories have faded out, swallowed whole by the trauma. I do remember being in the band at school starting around middle school, I guess. I also remember playing soccer and softball in elementary school. During those times, I made some dear friends, people I am still friends with to this day.

Some of them, like me, were abused quietly at home, too. That may have been the reason for some of our instant connections: always unspoken. Later in life, we would discuss some of the happenings from our home life back then. It is a kindred spirit and a kind word that made a huge difference and created a sense of belonging only the abused would understand.

Most of those kindred souls have really broken out of those abusive shells in their adult lives. It's a beautiful thing to see, knowing what they must've gone through back then, the courage and strength they had to have mustered to keep going and not give up fighting to become who they are now.

That's the real bitch in those times. Death seems like an unobtainable gift staring you in the face every morning when you look in the mirror. *If* you can stomach looking in the mirror at all.

Maybe that's how we survived: pushing aside all of the stuff and pretending it didn't exist in our little school world with our friends. Not looking in the mirror because we knew the deep sadness in our eyes would give our secrets away.

Making it out of high school without being arrested or killing anyone was a miracle in and of itself for me. Once I made it out of high school, I had no doubt I'd be dead or in jail by thirty if I didn't change something inside of me, if I didn't get this rage and hatred out of my soul. Guess that's what prompted the skydiving at age thirty.

During our childhood, our parents threw a party once a year at the end of tax season. Lots of people, lots of booze, lots of food. It was as if we lived a whole different life during those parties. Everyone smiled and hugged and enjoyed themselves. It was straight out of a fairytale. A life we could only dream about.

We all played our perfect little parts like good little soldiers. We knew what beatings awaited us if we didn't. Although it was definitely a nice reprieve from the abuse and the harshness of our reality.

Usually, some family would stay after the party, and we'd spend the next day doing the same thing with just extended family. I often wondered how none of them could see the abuse that was happening. Was it also happening to them? So it was an unspoken requirement to be in the family? The abuse had to be present? Sort of like the mafia? *This is just how it is, kid. Suck it up.*

Or did they already know the abuse was taking place and just couldn't stomach standing up to him or them or all of the abusers? There were three aunts on my dad's side; one died in a car accident early on in her life, probably trying to escape the horrors of their home life. Unfortunately for us, she was the most fun aunt. The other two were two completely different people even though they grew up in the same household. The abuse from their childhood was written all over their faces. I could see that even as a young child. I was never sure how much abuse they endured, but it was significant enough to warrant emotional eating and self-deprecating habits for each of their chosen paths in this life.

During our parents' divorce, those two remaining aunts made sure to tell us kids exactly what they thought of our mother. How much of a whore my mom was in high school, and how their family never liked her because she came from the poorer side of town. This, I feel, was at the behest of my father, who no doubt was still threatening them and a threat to them.

Mom and dad had already told us kids about how they met. I was the result of their first time in the backseat of a car. Her getting pregnant with me was the reason they were together. This fact would weigh heavily on me as the abuse continued, and my mom reminded me more often than not that I was the reason they are even together. Had I not been born into this world, maybe my brother, sister, and even my mom would have had much better lives.

I don't hold anything against my mom or these aunts now. In hindsight, they were being abused themselves and were probably doing as they were told by my father so as to avoid any additional abuse. Both aunts treated us as if we were second-rate citizens. In fact, all of the adults in my dad's family treated us this way.

Our clothes were never good enough. Our manners were never good enough. Our grades, our behavior, the way we combed our hair, the way we breathed, the way we ate, and on and on. Never. Good. Enough. In case we needed another constant reminder.

Again, as irony would have it, I am friends on social media with one of these aunts. The other aunt took things too far for me to consider even a distant relationship with her or her family. When I ask myself why I am allowing the one aunt to be in my world or still be "friends" with me, even on social media, my only thought is so she will know how well I turned out in this life. That I am not a fuck-up in this life. And that she has this same opportunity to be a different human, a better human, even late in her own life.

After my brother's death, my family all moved back to Mississippi. Me? I was stuck in Atlanta. I had big dreams and big plans. I was just trying to figure out how to get there from where I was. I think part of me was looking for a partner to make these big dreams and big plans successful, and I had no idea how to find that partner or even what to look for or what to do with him if I found him.

How could I? How could I possibly know what it took to make it all work? How could I even be considering burdening another human being with the task of making me whole again? How was it even their job to do so, even if they willingly agreed? How did I even have such big dreams and big plans from where I came from? What made me think I deserved any of that? What made me think I could make any of that happen for someone like me? I was reminded of this by my family anytime I got "too big for my britches," which basically meant they felt threatened by the pursuit of my own happiness.

Threatened because, on some level, it meant what they had provided for me wasn't good enough. It wasn't. But it was also the best they could give me with what they had to work with and the knowledge they possessed of this big, wide world. It wasn't their fault, nor was it mine. I had no hard feelings toward them for the life I had had. It was clearly a multigenerational, trauma-filled black hole that as yet none had dared to escape or expose.

During this early Atlanta adventure, I decided to go back to school even though I hated every bit of it. Back then, the belief was that you needed a college degree if you were going to amount to anything in this life. I set my mind to be more, even if it meant conformity. I was in and out of colleges, changing degrees, searching for some sort of silver lining of happiness. In and out of relationships, searching for the same thing. In and out of jobs, searching for one that felt right.

I was wild, bold, and audacious to the brink of self-destruction. Who cares? Clearly, I wasn't going to die anytime soon, or the plane jump would have answered my prayers. Right?

All I kept hearing in my head was, *Suck it up, buttercup.* As if this somehow made everything all better. Or helped me understand the path I was on.

After all that I had been through, my ego and arrogance stood up and said, *Bring it!* I wasn't afraid of death. In fact, I prayed for it. Every night when I went to bed, I prayed I wouldn't wake up the next morning. Some nights I even cried and begged that I would die in the night—I didn't even care how it happened. Robbers, rapists, fire, freak flood . . . whatever, just don't let me wake up tomorrow. In those moments, I didn't even care if others had to die with me. I just asked that my family have a better life after I was gone.

I was so deep in the spiral and so deeply entrenched in the Southern charm that hardly anyone even knew I was on the brink. There were only a few who could see the anger, rage, and desperation behind my eyes or hear it in my voice. I would risk anything: bar fights, bitch fights, whatever, *bring it!* I was not afraid, nor am I afraid now.

That I was raging mad is probably an understatement. I was raging mad because I was still alive and my brother wasn't. Raging mad because I didn't know what I could have done to make any of it turn out differently. Raging mad because the uncle and my dad were both running free, living their lives without shame or remorse for their actions. Raging mad because 99% of that was beyond my control. Raging mad because I couldn't allow anyone to get close enough to me to be burned to ash by the fire burning deep within my soul.

I wanted to fight. I wanted to die. And I didn't care what happened next.

More often than not, I considered just going into the bad part of town in Atlanta and disappearing. I was ten feet tall and bulletproof . . . only because I didn't give a fuck if I lived or died. I was alone now with all of the voices in my head telling me I wasn't good enough, smart enough, loving enough; if I were, my brother would still be alive, and I would still be married to the man I loved, and I could have made a difference, somewhere, somehow.

It was my fault. My "tough love" approach and my desire to be a millionaire by age thirty. I had abandoned my brother and probably my husband when they needed me the most. What good would those millions do me if everything and everyone I loved was gone? My brother's death was truly a breaking point for me.

Shortly after my brother's death, I abandoned my insurance clients, too. I went back to being a bartender. At least those fuckers *wanted* to see me, and I could mouth off to the biggest, meanest assholes and dared them to push me. Mind you, I was five-foot-four and weighed less than a buck then. Looking back, I'm sure it was quite comical to anyone who was watching. And probably equally as sad.

In hindsight, I definitely took some risks that clearly indicate to me now that there is a higher power. A source that kept me safe during those terribly bad decisions. Some decisions were worse than others, of course, but mostly, I made decisions that weren't in my best interest or in the interest of keeping myself safe or even alive. Once again I was torturing the little girl within, telling her she wasn't good enough to be saved, that she didn't deserve to be saved.

The relationships over these decades have also shown me that I am and have been both the recipient *and* the perpetrator of damage and hurt. I feel I have lived lifetimes as the giver and the receiver of trauma.

Caught up in the ebb and flow, giver and receiver of trauma, it is sometimes hard to see the damage I am causing or have caused. It can be hard to see how I'm perpetuating the deep, gaping wounds that would need to be tended and healed later. Some would call this closure. For me, it was always just another reminder of my shortcomings as a human being—as a woman.

It was never my intention to cause damage to another human just by being in a relationship with me. On some level the narcissistic patterns added to the passive-aggressive manipulations I learned from my father that fed my actions in my relationships. Until now, those patterns have not been truly recognized, acknowledged, or addressed. Unlearning that behavior as well as those behaviors built upon that false and shoddy foundation has been heavy, harder than I imagined, and also desperately lonely.

My judgment upon another human being, their actions, their feelings have all led me down a path of manipulation that I only realized within the past five years. With the flawed perfection of the lessons of my father, I was able to manipulate myself and also those caring human beings. In my past, I would have vehemently denied that I was anything like my father in terms of his manipulation tactics. I would have denied that I used someone's goodness or someone's feelings against them in times of anger—or, as irony would have it, times of not getting what I wanted out of a situation.

Within this loneliness, I have begun to find myself. My true self. On some level, it would seem beneficial to create a partnership with someone like myself. Someone who has been through their own trauma, who has chosen to heal their own past. A past of bullshit thrown at them from every angle, every corner, unable to control the speed, velocity, or accuracy of timing when those bullshit tapes of our past show up in our lives. The healing of those wounds must be at our own urging and at no one else's. An urging that comes from our own wounded inner child. Someone who now feels solid and grounded in who they are as a *whole* person.

It is challenging to stay in the feel zone as I write these pieces. I would rather run and hide, take a nap, or binge-watch something so I can avoid this uncomfortableness. Ironically, the uncomfortableness is much shorter lived if I face the demons head on rather than continuing to hide or run.

It also occurs to me, as I write these pieces, how much of my life I seemed to have "wasted." My mind begins to argue with itself at this point. I hear the old Eagles song about "Wasted Time" and agree with the thought process that leads me to the wasted time. How much time could I have spent not being angry, not feeling hurt about things that happened in the past, a past that I couldn't change and one that wasn't my fault?

In addition to the hurt and anger, I also never gave myself any credit. No credit for the trauma I endured, nor the adventures of a life well-lived in spite of all the pain. There were no celebrations of the good stuff, which was a travesty considering the encouragement it may have provided to propel me on to new adventures. It also leaves a feeling of "not-enough-ness" that has plagued me throughout my adulthood. And, if we are being honest, I can see these same patterns in my mother: constantly trying to "one-up" everything achieved in this life, rather than truly appreciating and being grateful for the beautiful, amazing life I am currently living.

Even in the midst of writing and feeling, the desire to reach for my phone and play a game or surf social media is strong. The degree of avoidance is very strong with this one. These demons are no joke. My brain is set to self-preservation—albeit self-preservation of an old pattern. An old pattern that has kept us alive and *sort of* thriving so far. The old pattern of not-enough-ness that pushes me to prove myself over and over again. To trust that I am good enough, to trust that I can handle anything that comes my way. One way or another.

In my decision to not have children of my own, I have become "cool Aunt Gel." And, sometimes "crazy Aunt Gel." Either are fine and accurate, honestly.

With this book, I worry what demons I may have inadvertently shared with these young souls as they crossed my path. For the most part, I avoid people at all costs when the demons are misbehaving. Sometimes that isn't possible. I have found that by sharing my secrets with other women, specifically, an immediate bonding is formed. Sometimes from their own history, sometimes from the nurturing that comes from being a strong woman. For the children, their laughter heals the world. As the cool aunt, my truest hope would be to be able to fill their self-esteem bucket so full it overflows onto everyone around them. Buckets, playgrounds, sidewalks, whole neighborhoods, spilling and covering all the world with the healing sound of laughter, bright light, love—that true, unconditional love—and acceptance. Some fun thrown in for good measure would be nice, too.

For those adults that passed like ships in the night, may they remember only the fun, the good times, and the laughter. For those adults and children I may have wronged somehow in this life, this is my earnest apology for not knowing better at the time. For not fighting for the deeply loving, caring, and kind little girl within, sooner. For not allowing her true self to shine sooner.

In this moment, I would also like to tell her that she was always worth fighting for—always worth saving. She deserved a better life than the one I have given her. But this is where we are now, who we are now.

Removing The Cloak

♥

I remember my grandparents telling me at a very young age that it was in my best interest to find a job and stick with it for thirty or forty years until I could retire and enjoy life. Even at my young age, I remember thinking what a terrible life that sounded like. Maybe it was the tone of despair in their voices. Maybe it was the naïveté of my young life. Even now, over age fifty, it still sounds terribly boring and unadventurous. Even with my Mississippi math skills, going to work at age eighteen and working for forty years doesn't leave much life to really enjoy.

The truth is, though, that I have stayed in the same line of work for the better part of thirty years, fulfilling those childhood expectations like the diligent and dutiful daughter that I am. During the times I attempted to venture off the well-beaten path laid out before me, others asked me, "What is wrong with you?" All the while, they dutifully did exactly what was expected of them.

What's wrong with me is that my heart bleeds with tears of a brutal past that no one knows or will ever admit happened. We are expected to "suck it up," "deal with it," "let the past go, it's over now anyway," fucking fill in the blank with the weighted blankets smothering the last remnants of life from our withering souls. A struggle to keep us all under control out of fear of exposing those secrets, bringing shame to the family. It is no wonder we dream of running wild and free, filling our physical bodies with tattoos and piercings, chasing physical pleasure and instant gratification at every turn—escapism at its very best.

With each stumble, we add the all-too-familiar overcompensating gesture to just be enough at that moment. Wondering if we will survive to the next, or if we even want to, all the while craving a life of our very own. We are told to pick a direction and stick with it. Do not go outside the box, do not color outside the lines, do not explore your curiosities, do not listen to your inner voice, or trust your instincts. Those things are for fools and poets.

Other than a therapist or two and my first husband, Jon, I have never shared my full story with anyone until the past few years. I finally decided it was time to shed the cocoon hiding my beautiful wings. Other damaged souls could already see them, anyway. They always found me, hiding in a corner, pretending to be normal and whole.

The level of exposure, courage, and vulnerability it takes to share your story, your darkest secrets with someone, is nearly indescribable. It's the feeling of taking a sip of water, in an attempt to quell the dehydrated, cotton-filled feeling in your mouth as you speak your truth; it's your mind flashing visions as the whole town throws stones at you while they parade you right through the middle of town, naked, barren, bleeding, everyone cursing your very existence. Until they finally dump you in the darkest, deepest well, never to be heard from again. The mighty sword of fear: a sure cure to prohibit any further nonsense such as this type of truth being spewed from any other human.

As the words come out of your mouth, the visions subside. The room is quiet except for the tears you are unable to weep but are spilling from the eyes of those who heard you. They heard you. They felt you. They didn't shun you, and they didn't leave you. What kind of magic of humanity is this?

As you take a breath, you experience an uncomfortable feeling. One you have never felt before. How could you have felt this relief, this release? This is that time now for you to release your truth and feel the grief leaving out of your soul, so your wings can fully extend into your life.

The freedom to just be who I am. To be without shame from a past that wasn't my fault: that is true freedom. I was able to genuinely *be*, and each time I tell my story now, those around me feel free to share their stories. The reconciling of the wrongs and the truth are a medicinal salve covering the souls of long-kept secrets. It feels like fresh air finally reaching the deep crevices that have been long covered by the shame and guilt.

In telling my story, I gained a freedom of self, allowing me to be me now. I am no longer living someone else's definition of success. In pursuing this journey to find my own soul, my own voice, I have made choices that only a few will ever understand.

I have been released from the adult-induced, self-inflicted restrictions caused by a childhood that I could not accept, proclaim, or liberate myself from . . . until now. Now, taking calculated risks to show my true colors has allowed me to use my voice for the first time in my life. Calculated risk is an attempt of my rational mind to justify the new adventures ahead.

I am removing the cloak while holding tightly to the daggers in each hand. Still, I am ready to fight at a moment's notice. It is better now as at least I am no longer fighting myself or the little girl within. I'm better in the sense that I have gained some clarity on this journey, some hope, some joy. And, most importantly, I've gained some peace.

About a year ago, I bought a motorcycle and joined a group of women riders. Most of these women are around my same age, and clearly, they share some of the same life traumas.

During what they call an "overnighter," I was brave enough to share my story with a few of them. This is essentially a forty-woman sleepover. It was an amazing experience, and our common ground allowed us to be open and unrestricted with one another.

Riding my motorcycle stirs within me a pure desire to experience life as I have always imagined it could be. That young girl, back in Atlanta, ready to take on the world, knowing it is about to be the best it has ever been.

Within the past three years, I have also moved nearly 2,000 miles away from my family "home." It wasn't until I visited out here that I understood the word "majestic." We all sang the song in elementary school, but to see these mountains, to feel these mountains, you can feel the word filling up your very soul.

Being out here in the wild, wild west feeds my own soul. It's the most "at-home" I have ever felt. It is no place for the weak, no place for anyone who is not a survivor, lest you disappear. Out here in the unforgiving landscape, as time pounds out a beating on the mountainous skyline in a cruel juxtaposition, everything seems within reach and far away all at once. You're close enough to slide your fingertips across the roughness, feeling its soft underbelly seep into your soul.

Over the recent six months, I have also taken another giant step toward that freedom of self. I took a much needed break from the industry that has been my anchor for thirty years. I find no humor in the fears that arise from these new freedoms. My path is unsteady, uncharted, but at least it is all mine now. I am no longer pushing all of my own buttons, firing on all ten cylinders at all times in an effort to maintain the facade of normalcy. I've made a commitment to myself, accepting the flaw in the perfection that is me. I will no longer be held back from delivering my best version of myself, the grandest version of the greatest vision I can hold.

Although this latest journey is certainly not without risk, reward, or grief, I must allow the flow . . . of time, of healing, and of shedding this skin of shame at my own pace. Allowing time for myself, time to grieve the loss of a life I haven't yet lived, time to grieve the perceived wrong choices made along the way, all while denying the truth. Time for allowing the anger of the shoulda, woulda, couldas of my past. All of the "what-ifs" fade into the darkness because they no longer belong to me. I'm allowing myself to be "depressed." I'm sleeping longer than I should, watching movie after movie, avoiding my reality, eating and drinking ad nauseam, ceaselessly, unhealthily. I'm negotiating with myself for my own freedom—if I do this, then I can do this; if I say this, then I can feel this. Maybe if I just wait this out long enough, everything will work out. If I just dress like this, think like this, speak like this . . . all will work out in my favor.

I'm attempting to accept me as I am now. The flawed perfection of a human being. Trauma-filled childhood aside, adult choices gone awry, survival and handle-it mode finally receding, I'm allowing my body to sink into the floor, emancipated from the bondage of my shame.

The weekend-long, seemingly endless rivers of tears I have shed in the past were worth it to get me here. Now, I stand firmly in the arena of my life—my own life, a life I am actively, compassionately, eyes-wide-open-ly choosing for myself.

Fuck all those motherfuckers. This is my shit show.

Healing In The Exposure

🖤

W ay *back in the* day, before cell phones had cameras, there were cameras with actual film inside. This film was sensitive to the light. Once exposed to the light, the pictures were ruined. The stories those pictures told would never be able to be recovered, hidden away for all of time. There was no hope once it was exposed to the light.

Now, with the World Wide Web, it is just the opposite. Once exposed on the web, there is no taking it back, *ever*. It is out there for all of eternity and for all to see.

Both of these options hold their own set of good and bad. On the one hand, those pictures were lost forever in the film days, but you still had those memories. They were yours alone to have, to hold, and relive anytime, even if they were bad. These days, there are no take-backs. Once something is out there on the web, especially if it's bad, it's there forever.

Fear of exposure is what kept those film canisters closed and safe back in the day. That, and they were good for your pot stash because they sealed in the smell and seemed harmless for any looky-loos. That's a story for another day, though.

My story of generational trauma is a lot like that old film. Or, at least, I thought it was. If I told my truth, exposed my true, raw, soft underbelly, I would be ruined. I'd need to hide away for all of time. The weight of the shame, the weight of the pity that was sure to follow such exposure, would be too much to bear. Maybe that's why it has taken me so long to really share my story. I have lived this long without exposing the truth of my life publicly, but I can no longer hold it in. The weight of my story, of my truth, is too heavy now. Too heavy for my physical body and much, much too heavy for my emotional body. I need somewhere else for it to go. I can no longer stuff it down inside.

In all of the years of therapy, all of the years of crying myself to sleep at night, all of the years of putting on my game face and handling shit, not once have I told all of the truth of my story.

Why should I? Why can't I just let it go and move on? It is all in the past anyway, right?

But it follows me. It haunts me in every moment of every day. My tough exterior armor won't allow anyone close enough to hurt me again, and it also keeps out those who truly want to love me right here and now for the woman I am becoming; the ones that want to love me as if I were never broken. I feel that my truth is all over my face, and that truth shows in how I walk, how I talk, how I sit, how I interact with the whole world. Those with trauma of their own always seem to gravitate toward me, as if I am somehow a beacon, and I toward them without even realizing I have any light left shining.

How do you hide in plain sight? More importantly, how long can I keep this up?

I am exhausted from all of the pretending to be okay, the pretending that life is perfect and lovely, and I am a badass. In all fairness, I am a badass for all that I have accomplished in this life in spite of the trauma of my childhood. It doesn't change the fact that I am too exhausted to keep up the charade

now, and I need to share the truths in all of my many
stories . . .

This is not a want. This is an absolute *need*. I am now
willing to take that risk of exposure to shine the light of my
truth. I need to know if I am safe or if I am headed to the
slaughter. A slaughtering of my life, a slaughtering of my
reputation, of my very being. I have built and conquered
through a facade of okay-ness through it all. My fear was
always that this facade would disappear in my telling of my
truth, of my trauma, and of my story.

It is a scary thing to stand alone and speak your truth. It is
a palm-sweating, dry-mouth, suffocating, and gasping-for-air
moment that drags on like a slow-motion clock, ticking your
life away down to the final explosion. We tend to believe the
explosion will be a big bang propelling us into a wide-open
space, like skeet waiting for the sound of the rifle fire. All the
while, we're silently screaming, *NO! I am not ready!*

But the truth is, I am ready. I am in need of the exposure—
even at the risk of getting shot into a million pieces like a skeet
disc.

In my usual—all-in or all-out—approach to life, I took this
chance during a forty-woman sleepover with my motorcycle
friends, albeit in the safety of my own vehicle with only a few
of those women within earshot. I hadn't planned this exposure.
Why would I? Even with these strong, badass women who
have endured as much life as me, why would I risk it now that I
finally feel I have found my tribe?

Because it was time. It was time I took a chance on myself.
A chance on them. These are a bunch of badass biker chicks
with their own life stories. Who was I to show up as the new

gal and drop this on them? My decision was not made from fear or "I must do this." No, it was made from a place of my own safety within myself, my own knowing that it was time. In my mind, though, it was definitely too risky here. I didn't know them, and they didn't know me, but . . . I guess that's the point of the sleepover, right?

In writing this book, reliving the intimate details of these experiences has brought up so much that just a year ago I would have told you I had already let go of it all. That I had already healed it and moved on.

Not even close. Not. Even. Close.

Can you really just let go of the image of yourself you have carried your whole life? I've held on so tightly to the lies I have believed for decades now. *Not good enough. No one is going to believe you. Everyone is going to hate you. You will never be good enough for anyone. No one is ever going to truly love you.* Those aren't things you just wake up and decide to toss out like a pair of worn-out shoes. These are forever shoes. Like a pair of hand-made Italian leather sandals that fit so perfectly you aren't even sure you're wearing shoes. That is how comfortable we become with the tapes of our abusers, of our childhood, and of those meant to love and care for us most.

It was a Saturday, and four of us decided to drive into town for some shopping. I volunteered to drive knowing I had four-wheel drive and snow tires and faith in my little Jeep to get us out of whatever situation. During this time, most places required masks due as a precaution against COVID. I had to be open and honest about that, too, as I am unable to wear a mask because it causes severe panic attacks, most likely from PTSD from my childhood.

Until this COVID stuff, I had no idea that wearing a mask would cause me to have panic attacks, although I never liked to wear the plastic masks at Halloween, either. The only other times I felt panic setting in have been in elevators with too many people, and I am not a fan of crowded rooms or big gatherings; I never have been. There are too many risk factors there. I am also the person that sits with their back to the wall in the restaurant, facing the door.

This psychological trickery I play with myself out of my need to feel some sense of control over my life. Facing the door, at least I can see trouble when it walks in, right? At least that is what I tell myself. Facing the door (literally and metaphorically), I can pretend to relax now.

These women were all prepared with their masks, and I had to come clean about my panic attacks. This, too, is a vulnerable place to be. Their response could have been one much less compassionate, much less caring. They were all very understanding and accepting of me and my panic attacks.

We had to leave one shop because the shop owner was non-compassionate about my plight of anxiety. I felt bad because they missed an opportunity because of me, and it looked like a cool shop. On the other hand, that shop owner also lost out on possible sales from bored, well-funded, badass women.

On the drive back to our bunkhouse, someone asked about the panic attacks. Not so much about the panic attacks themselves, but *why* I have panic attacks. The words were releasing themselves from the stronghold of a tongue that had long forgotten it was a choice to speak. My words were flying free like a bird just released from its cage.

"Trauma," I said quietly. "Trauma from my childhood. Abuse on all levels. Mental, psychological, physical, emotional, and sexual abuse from those who were supposed to protect me most."

As I continued, the rising up of my shoulders ceased, and my shoulders dropped square, my jaw tightening, waiting for the fatal blow. I tightened my torso for the gut punch surely on its way, weight balanced and steady, chin tucked into my chest, with both hands up for protection and deflection. I awaited the blow that was sure to come after exposing my truth.

Realizing what was happening within my own body, I took a deep breath. A slow, ragged breath. Air trapped within my tiny lungs released softly. My tiny lungs filled with decades of grief and sadness. I released the defensive boxer pose, lowering my fists from their secure stronghold of my torso and face. Adjusting my breathing, I opened my body, my mind, and my soul to these badass women—knowing on some deep level, I was safe.

There was no turning back now. It was out on the table anyway.

The weight of the energy in the Jeep felt as if it would flatten all four tires at once. A complete and total blowout on the snow-covered roads caused us to slide off and roll side over side into the pile of trees dated 1989 by the forest service.

I was expecting them to gasp and not speak the rest of the trip. I was prepared to be dismissed from the group as soon as we arrived back at that bunkhouse; surely, they wouldn't allow me to stay. They were obviously pensively and silently thinking how fucked up I must be, and how they had to spend another night in an open bunkhouse with this crazy, PTSD-inflicted, damaged, broken human. No fucking way! How could they possibly allow someone who is just blabbering all of their shit out like that? Over-sharer was an understatement at this point; there were no take-backs now.

It was exposed. I was exposed.

I'd assumed they were probably thinking, *She looks normal, but obviously she isn't. She could come unhinged at any moment. We don't know her. She might be dangerous in her damaged state. Had she confronted and maybe even killed those who violated her, killed those who broke her trust, or betrayed her? What if one of us makes her mad or triggers her in some way? How can we sleep tonight with her just feet away from us, knowing we know her shame now? Her shame that she's hidden behind this facade of normalcy, pretending, posing as a normal human who just likes to ride motorcycles. How dare she!*

But none of that happened.

The Jeep and her tires moved smoothly and elegantly along the snow-covered roads with ease.

Someone from the back spoke up and said softly, "Me, too."

Another in the back agreed, and she began telling a piece of her story. "It is no wonder we are kindred spirits," she said.

A soft sigh of relief released itself from my lungs as I realized these strong, beautiful, badass women were my tribe. On some level, having gone through their own trauma, there was no way our souls weren't vibrating toward each other on this trajectory called life.

The elephant had now been lifted off my chest. If I had been honest with myself, I could have admitted that I could feel the damage from these women before I ever spoke. Even the ones with "perfect childhoods" had the damage on their soul, like a beacon drawing me to these ladies. These women are strong, dedicated, and deliberate creators of their own lives, raising strong, determined daughters. This is a tribe of fighters. My tribe. Strong, but damaged. Like me. I stepped out on that limb with my arms splayed wide—HERE I AM—and they caught me.

Since that time, more and more of these women have shared their trauma stories with me. Most of us look so normal, so put-together, handling shit like badass adults who love to ride motorcycles. The freeing of ourselves in the exposure of our trauma, to each other, to the safety of non-judgmental "I got you" women. One even said she had never told anyone and wasn't sure what made her tell us then. It is the energy of the telling, the healing in the exposure, that causes us to reach out for the healing, reach out for the acceptance, reach out for the compassion, strength, and friendship.

The Ebb And
Flow of Healing

♥

N o one ever tells us how long it will take to heal. The reason is it's different for each person and our own unique guidance system in this life. (Read: this is YOUR healing, it takes as long as it takes). I can also tell you that no one even talks about how long the "processing" of trauma and healing will take. This, too, is an individual journey with many twists and turns. It's not linear. It will always take more time and energy than you are prepared to endure. On the edge of giving up, that is the place you find peace, if you just keep going.

For me, I never realized how much time I needed to just sit with the things that have happened to me. I was (and am) headstrong. I've got a let's-get-this-done-and-move-on attitude. My therapists and well-meaning friends would try to tell me it doesn't work like that, but I never listened.

"I will do it differently," said every strong-willed child in the history of mankind. "It is different for me." We can continuously stream vomited words that are meaningless to us because, at the end of the day, we just want so desperately to be on the other side of the trauma and into the healing. Therapists and the like will tell us it will be "hard work" to get through to the healing. And we don't believe that, either. At least I didn't.

Hard work doesn't scare me. My life is a perfect example of that. There are no words of consolation to ease the pain of the hard work of which they speak. And they speak the truth.

It *is* scary. Sometimes it feels as if you are drowning, sinking to the bottomless pit of those who have struggled in their own families to end the generations of trauma and abuse. The bottomless pit of "see, it can't be done" that society has taught us is what happens when you push against the grain.

There are also those of us who have suffered trauma that weren't so fortunate as to have the strength of a support system pushing or supporting them. There are those of us who have died in vain, waiting for a failed system to "save us." Case in point: those useless temporary restraining orders (TROs), which are humiliating in themselves just to file. And this is coming from a woman. I can't even imagine what it must be like for a man to need to file one.

The level required by law to prove you've been threatened or are in fear of your life is there for a reason, I suppose. And it would probably be okay except that the piece of paper, once served to the violator, tends to evoke the opposite response, resulting in even further damage, assault, and sometimes death.

With assault, there's also the issue of the statute of limitations. For instance, in my case, when I was a child, no one pressed charges against my abusers. As an adult, I could have pursued charges. However, the burden of proof would have been on me as an adult, proving I was assaulted as a child nearly a decade earlier.

The entire system and process seem hopeless and in vain, resulting in opening wounds best left closed. The dull, rusted blade of that knife opening those wounds would only cause sepsis, and as such, attack the entire physical, emotional, and psychological body of the already wounded, and possibly result in death. Reports of the abuser even "finishing off" their victims once they were exposed are rampant, as are suicides among those abused. Sometimes, the abusers themselves get off easy by taking their own lives, too. Talk about leaving a gaping wound without closure; therapists could clean up in this arena. A lot of days are spent in hopeless despair because there aren't any real answers for victims of assault, abuse, and trauma. There is no closure.

What is there to do now? Just wallow through it as best you can. *Suck it up, buttercup. Too bad for you. We all had it rough at some point in our lives. It is what it is, kid . . . get over it. Move on.*

There have been those who have fought hard to bring their abusers to justice. (Think Anita Hill Corey Feldman, for starters) There have been steps made in psychotherapy, including hypnosis and repressed memory techniques, to aid in proving the case against the abuser. Again, it is seemingly dusted under the rug, touted as psycho-babble gibberish conjured up by some greedy lawyer. But is that really the case?

Most days, I am a well-functioning adult. I'm holding down a great job in an industry I've worked in for three decades now. I have a home and good clothes, my bills are paid, and I have a smile on my face. The smile is a reminder that better days are ahead, there is a light, and that this time, it isn't a train. I'm a perfect example of a law-abiding, never-been-arrested, compassionate, kind, intelligent, and well-put-together human. Nothing to see here. Move along quietly.

Then, on seemingly random other days, that caged animal ready for a fight comes raging back in with a vengeance. Thoughts of forming a vigilante group that targets sexual predators, especially child molesters, fill every corner of my mind, body, and soul. My body is tight with anger, my back straight, shoulders squared, jaw clenched, solar plexus taut. My fingernails dig into my palms as my hands ball into the tightest fists, ready for a battle to the death.

A welcomed death, one providing a false sense of satisfaction in serving justice upon those who intentionally and knowingly inflict pain on another. Splattering their blood all over the battlefield of life, putting their skulls on sticks in the front yard for the world to see. As a sign for both those they abused to know justice had been served but also for those leaning toward that same seedy path of harming another to know what fate awaited them.

But . . . but . . . wait! I am a good human! I am not violent! I am a peace-loving gypsy with a "do as ye wish, harm none" view on this life. How can I possibly even consider causing intentional pain on another, even if they are a bad human? At that point, I, too, would become a bad human.

This juxtaposition leads most of us to question our own sanity and resolve. Why keep fighting? It is a useless fight. Nothing will ever be done, and I will never be at peace. Discussing these thoughts with a therapist could mean time in an institution, although sometimes that also feels like a potential relief of the burden. You could write in a journal, but make sure you burn that shit later—can't have anyone finding it accidentally. Or you could discuss it with your closest and dearest. But the shame and the fear of judgment and rejection are just too great. It's best to leave well enough alone and go on pretending.

I feel the truth of the matter is that this is the ebb and flow of trauma and of healing. How could it not be so? There are those of us who have created a beautiful life for ourselves in spite of the trauma we have endured. Even within that beautiful life, there are things that provoke those inner demons, such as a smell, a word, or an action by someone who may be oblivious to our journey before that moment. The spiral down is swift like a staircase slathered in that Southern bacon grease from on top of Grandma's stove—and headed straight to hell.

At times, this happens before we even realize it. Worse yet, there is hardly any time to step back and redress the freshly opened wound. A wound oozing with newly exposed and long-infected pus from our past rushing toward the light. No, this usually happens at those times when we've made commitments that must be kept. They must be kept in order to keep our facade intact.

Should we falter now, everyone would know we were damaged and possibly broken. This perceived faltering would also cause them to steer clear of us because now, we also cannot be counted on as reliable, and we cannot be trusted.

That's when it is a good time for the vigilante visions to show up. At least if you went off the rails, it would be expected that you would be an unreliable, untrustworthy, dangerous, and a "crazy" person. If that's what everyone already thinks, it is easier just to be that. No fancy clothes necessary!

So how do we maintain some level of normalcy, of functionality in our lives, and carry these burdens? How do we not become monsters in this life seeking vengeance on all who have wronged us or someone we love? Is religion the answer?

Seek God first, and everything will work out? That might work for some. It did not work for me, although I did try it in earnest.

After decades of searching for something that will help, I am still searching. I can tell you that it must be a daily practice to remain human, to care, to be compassionate and kind and loving. The harsh reality of every day will feed on the demons of our past unless we control our thoughts and emotions.

We must focus or redirect our attention daily on the good in our current lives. We must find a way to be gentle, kind, and compassionate toward ourselves, which, for me, has been the hardest journey yet. We must allow ourselves however long it takes for us to heal. If we can redirect that focus and energy in our lives, we can function and heal simultaneously. The two are not mutually exclusive. However, it will require nurturing ourselves above all else. Not in a selfish, not-going-to-feed-my-kids-today-because-I-am-having-a-meltdown way, but in a let's-feed-the-kids-and-take-a hot-bath-and-cry-to-release-this-dis/ease.

We must make an effort to look for the good in each day, in each moment, using our keen focus and all of our senses to fill our days and nights with things that bring us joy and make us smile, lest the demons take us.

It sounds so cliché and New-Agey, but it is, in fact, the only thing that has kept me sane. And now that my story has been exposed, I am truly free to push back on a society that has no room for healing, no room for exposing the truth. *Just keep moving forward. Nobody has time for that nonsense.* That's what they say. That's what they tell us. Whether they believe it themselves or not.

Maybe it isn't cliché or New-Agey at all. Maybe that is the lie they told us to believe so that we would sit down, shut up, and do our fucking jobs. *Stop whining about your tough childhood and needing a hot bath or time to yourself. Handle it.*

On this journey of late with the writing of this book, my identity crisis seems to have turned toward questioning how many times I have done or said something that prompted another human to slip down their own greased staircase. More importantly, how do I not do it again? Take a moment to reflect on the words we say, the colloquialisms we use in our daily lives that stem from repression or oppression of another, or the socially acceptable put-downs with undertones of how weak and useless women are. We might need a whole new fucking language. And when did this become acceptable?

Relationships
After Trauma

*R*elationships in general have always been challenging for me. They've been a sordid attempt at wholeness from a broken past. I find myself searching for something or someone who would ease the angst of my buckshot-filled soul.

As the oldest child, for the most part, I was treated like a boy. The assumption was that I was (obviously) a tomboy at heart. I mean, we *did* live in Mississippi, so it kind of makes sense. In most situations, I was expected to hold the door for the women and children, carry the heavy stuff into the house, and generally do the "male" duties. I was expected—or I felt it was expected of me—to protect those same women and children. Even today, I much more fiercely protect the women and children around me, and I am quick to step up to the plate should I feel someone has wronged one of them.

This behavior created more than one battlefield for me in the relationship department. On the one hand, it was an obvious challenge to the actual men in the near vicinity. Which, in all honesty back then, just made me raise the bar higher in a full-on peacock dance to the death.

As if that wasn't enough, it has sometimes led others to label me as a lesbian—the butch version. In fact, one of my very first published articles was about women back in the mid-nineties and how much we have endured and overcome. About how you can see the life a woman has lived if you watch her carefully. Her eyes, her movements, her soul will show itself to you if you just watch, without judgment, as the beauty of that woman unfolds before your very eyes.

My own mother, along with a few others, asked me if I was a lesbian after that article. Um, no.

This sort of thinking is exactly what I am talking about. We, as women, were taught that it was "wrong" or something sexual in nature if we nurtured and cared for each other. It made me angry then, and it makes me angry now. What are they so afraid of if we actually care for each other?

Two women roommates. In the minds of most, that means there is or was some sort of hanky-panky going on there. Or maybe it's wishful thinking of those men in the know. And this is definitely true in the minds of most men when they imagine two women "living together." Are we seriously this shallow as a society? I feel this is the epitome of too much male domination in our society. I am not a feminist in the political sense; however, there are clear incidents such as this that cannot be mistaken for anything other than the male undertone and overtone that it is. It almost always leads back to sexuality. I say not a feminist because I somehow still believe in a perfect balance in this world. Balance is the key, young Padawan. And also, what's good for the goose is good for the gander.

As women, it would seem we are forced to struggle to find our balance, sexually speaking. Back in the fifties, we were expected to be the perfect housewife and mother with no other life outside of that, no other interests in this world other than our husbands, our children, and our home. As we rolled into the sixties (literally and figuratively), women began to be more free. But we were shunned by those who weren't considered "hippies." Even if we moved through such a phase, we were branded by society. Like a bright, scarlet letter letting the world know for sure we were free-loving, loose women. Never mind all the men who also partook in those festivities; no, they weren't shunned or labeled, at all. They were virtually exalted to sainthood in our society. What the fuck is wrong with this picture? Is it just me?

Edging out of the sixties and into the early seventies, we, as a nation, are at war. Somehow, it was okay now that strong women were standing up. Standing up and fighting for our country, fighting for their families. Hey, progress is progress, right? This is about when I showed up to the party.

By the mid-seventies, life as a woman definitely began to shift. And here we are. I am thankful for these strong, badass women who came before me and pushed those boundaries for themselves. But they also pushed them for those of us who came during and after. They kicked out the ends of the grave meant to bury us—as women. Conformity was and always has been, the killer.

I have no doubt, as I write this, this time was equally as challenging for the males of our species. Where do they fit in our new paradigm? If they are not our great panacea, now they, too, must find a new way to be. And thus the battle for control, evident in the past few decades, much like that first year of marriage.

The lopsidedness of our society today is due to this power struggle, I feel. I hear Dr. MLK asking, "Can't we all just get along?" Well, yes, of course we can . . . sort of. A two-headed snake isn't good for anybody. There must be balance. There must be allowance and acceptance but not necessarily reparations or requirements of one to be fully immersed in the other. Acceptance of another human's point of view. Allowance of another human's way of life. Period. Given my native heritage, this is challenging to accept. Then, I hear JFK: "Ask not what your country can do for you, ask what you can do for your country." Two brave men gunned down in their heyday. And now, John Lennon and "Imagine." Imagine what these two men would have accomplished in our world had they been allowed, had they been accepted, had there been balance in place of the fear.

I remember my studies in Atlanta at the Ahimki Center for Wholeness. Catherine had to give us her dissertation. She stood so boldly in front of us all and spoke of a deep, long, abiding love of Raef. For as long as I live, I will never forget her or her presentation that day. She spoke of Raef as someone who had not only touched her soul but someone who would never, ever leave her, someone who stood steadfastly by her side at all times. Each morning Raef was a constant companion as she awoke, with her each moment as she went on about her day, visiting her at lunch, and again at dinner while she dined alone or with others. As she concluded her presentation, she flipped the letters around. Raef=FEAR. Holy shit! I am pretty sure I spent the next few days in shock. Shock because, I, too, was in love with Raef as she spoke of him. He was so familiar, so attached to my very being. In the end, I knew exactly who Raef was, and I did not like it one bit. Harsh, but accurate. Now, it is time to release Raef like your worn-out, favorite pair of shoes that now make your feet hurt as you travel down the new roads in your new life.

Dreaming of the perfect relationship takes so much to get me to a place of openness, of vulnerability. I am afraid my liver will fail before I accept what my heart cannot, before I accept the whole of who I am in this life. I ask myself, often, who would willingly join this shit show? And, the same coin, meeting new contestants, I find myself wondering if this man before me is strong enough to endure what lies ahead.

Fine, yes, I am aesthetically pleasing and my outward cheerleader facade does wonders for everyone around me. What happens then, when in our alone time, the vulnerable, soft Angel shows up? I can already tell you. All of them *run*! And they run as fast and as far as they can get. Who can blame them, though, really? I showed up one way and behind closed doors, I am sometimes a different person that needs the touch, the cuddles, and their own cheer squad.

This, this is not for the weak or tender-hearted, although that is exactly how my own heart feels on most days. Weak and tender, and in need of love, kindness, nurturing, and a place to heal. Maybe that's what we all need and long for.

I am tired. I am weak. I am in need of a reprieve. Someone to wage the battle while I rest knowing that this human and I are both doing our very best, the absolute. The absolute best that I myself would give to this battlefield of life—the battlefield we are both fighting to survive.

I must push away these down, out, and negative thoughts from my mind. It takes work, effort, perseverance, and consistency. I deserve an amazing life. I deserve someone who loves me for me, for what I have survived, for what I am becoming, and I deserve a long and beautiful thirty-plus years with this amazing human. And no matter how many times it takes, I must be brave and open my heart again and again and again, without ever really knowing why or if I should.

Sometimes, I think finding a mate is kind of like choosing the perfect avocado. You pick one that looks aesthetically pleasing, feel around for the soft spots, knowing full well there will be a few bruises, but it's probably okay. It is only after you get it home and cut it open that you realize just how deep the bruises of their own life reach. Then it's already cut open. Now you have to do something with it or throw it away.

The questions then become deeper, more entrenched in the life of and in the potential of a life together. If you choose to move forward in doing something with the bruised and damaged part, it seems important that they, too, are already working on healing those wounds. If they are not, then we, as wounded souls ourselves, find ourselves in a place of wanting to "fix" things. Fix things for this human, fix things for the past, present, and future of this human. But if they weren't ready to fix these things for themselves before you showed up, what makes you think they are ready now?

Which leaves "throw it away." Sounds extremely harsh in that terminology. That makes it seem as if there were something viable at some point along the way in this journey together. If the bruises are that deep, and they have not begun to heal and work on themselves, was there really anything viable? It's a harsh lesson for me, as I find it challenging to leave humans who are good overall but have some trauma that needs to be healed. I find myself wanting to stick around and help them. It is hard for me to accept that someone can't see or doesn't want to see their own trauma, to heal and move forward. Forward into a better, more satisfying life. Communication is a biggie. If someone never learned to communicate without bashing another person, that is not communication. That is abuse. An easy fix with a little patience and therapy, but sometimes too much to swallow and too deep a pattern to simply allow it to flow away, allowing love to take its place. So many relationships today could be healed and could be amazingly beautiful with proper communication. Learning to love each other right here, right now, and through the trauma we now know we have all endured on some level.

Back in the nineties, I had my astrological chart read by a well-renowned astrologer in Atlanta. She was a fantastic human and a little spitfire, too. Lyn told me a lot of things over those few readings, two of those I remember very well. One was that I am here to "do something big by just getting the word out," and the other was that I am an "honorary Scorpio." Writing this book feels like my something big to me, but I can't be sure. The honorary Scorpio part: I knew exactly what that was about. My sexuality.

With a broad, general, stereotypical paintbrush . . . I can say that most girls with my past chase father figures for approval. I chased passive-aggressive males in hopes of approval but it was my mother's approval that I secretly wanted, not my father's. But I chased these men with the aggressiveness I learned from my Scorpio father. Oh, the irony of that chase.

As an honorary Scorpio, my "rockstar" persona was assured on all levels of this life. Without even trying, honestly. I was on an adventure to make people feel good, smile, laugh— even if it was at me and my antics—and then leave while I was on top. Seemed like a smart business model, except for those times when I didn't leave because I was having too much fun. Or because I hadn't convinced enough people in the room that I was, indeed, a rockstar. If only I had believed that about myself back then . . . imagine the mountains I could have moved!

Again, back to that wasted time piece of this puzzle. #latebloomer

I walked into most rooms as if I owned the place. (Pretend-confidence is almost as believable as the real thing, as long as people don't look too deeply or stick around for too long.) Every insecure woman in the room moved closer to her man and held on tight. Back in my twenties, I found this delightful, although I had no idea what to do with it. Now, in my fifties, I find it sad that these women feel so insecure in their relationships. The irony is that insecure men want to shame me into submission. Hide me from the world, force me into conformity, long skirts, long sleeves, and never leave the house without their escort—yep, perfect relationship right there . . . insert eye roll here. As if crushing the very essence of who I am as a woman somehow makes them feel more like a man, or makes them love me more or even the same. Sounds legit.

My stepdad will tell you a story about those times that was one of his favorites. There was a neighborhood guy who worked for one of my mom's friends. I said he was gay. My stepdad asked how I knew. I said something to the effect of, "He didn't flinch when I walked into the room." This was my barometer.

Attention, it would seem, was something I slightly craved at those times. Although, once the spotlight shined on me, unless it was about insurance, I froze like a deer in headlights, standing on the edge of the highway in the backwoods of

Mississippi with a .30-06 pointed right at my rapidly beating heart.

Another friend of mine from Miami used to tell me I wasn't allowed to go to Miami alone. When I asked why, he would tell me because I was too gullible. Albeit, he had some good sales tactics, he would throw crazy stuff in there just to see how far I would believe him. I was so angry to be thought of as gullible, but also, I wanted to learn how not to be so obvious, predictable, or so easily taken advantage of. Ultimately, in this life, I am this gullible, and he was right. Somehow this saddens, frustrates, and also angers me.

In my late forties and now into my fifties, I can't help but wonder if this "rockstar persona" has been a blessing or a curse, or both. How do I rein it in and use it for good? Have I used it for good in the past? Or was it all for self-flagellation and repeated torture of my very own soul and the little girl inside?

Over the years, some passing women have even told me to "rein it in," to "rein my energy in," so that I could have a better life. My only question was, "A better life by whose definition?" Or was it simply to alleviate their own affront to my very existence? Something for which, I feel, neither of us are to blame. Is this larger than life energy I exude a deterrent to my relationships, in general? And, with both males and females?

Is it possible the men in this world had no idea either? Were they simply relying on fear as their only guide in this life? Is that where we have all gone wrong? Allowing Raef to swallow us in a complete surrender? These are the ponderings of a healing soul wishing for healing of all others along the way.

Two of my very best friends in all the land . . . one is a Scorpio, like my father, and one is an Aquarius, like my mother. "Balance, young Padawan" is all I can hear. And, also, irony. How is it that all of these years, I couldn't really get along with either of my parents, but I get along with these two badass, fierce women?

They have accepted me for me during lots of trials and tests—intentional and unintentional. I am unable to find words for my gratitude to them and their steadfastness with me, this journey, my journey. Again, irony for a writer to have no words.

This brings me to judgment. Mostly, my own judgment of my actions in this life. Especially when it comes to sex, love, sensuality, and relationships. Most of my girlfriends would tell me that I move too fast. We've been through the "why" already. Some of my girlfriends would tell me to be free, to be me—sexy, sensual, and free on all levels. Sometimes, it was a definite, *What have I done now?* And sometimes it was an, *Oh, this could work.* We've been through this before though, too, right? I have no concept of what slow and what fast look like within a relationship. I roll with my feelings, my desires, and allow the chips to fall where they may. Chaos and uncertainty are dear old friends. Much life Raef.

Ironically, the ones who had me thinking, *What have I done?* are the ones who wanted to stay. Those who had me thinking, *This could work.* Those, those are the ones who couldn't get to the door fast enough to get away from me. Even if they stayed around for a bit . . . for no other reason than because the honorary Scorpio sex was good. Wink wink.

As a young girl, I remember reading my dad's Playboy magazines. I am not sure why, other than they were so "taboo" back in the seventies and eighties. Maybe it was for the articles. Again, wink wink.

My annual checkups have been fun past age forty, as well. The female docs always begin their exam and tell me how much different my cervix looks since I haven't had children— this also means no episiotomy. Menopause also came early for me. A blessing and a curse.

It's a blessing because now, I can have as much fun as I want without concern of causing another human the past I endured. A curse because I can have as much fun as I want, but I will never be able to show my own child that life can be different, different and better than the one I endured.

A blessing and a curse, much like my sexuality in general. A blessing during the truly confident times, a curse during the times when I questioned life itself and my existence in it.

There was a time when I was a huge flirt. Maybe that was the bartender coming out in me, as a way to make a living. These days, the term is salty . . . or sass mouth. All of the above are accurate, fortunately or unfortunately. But that depends upon who you ask. And in case you were wondering, yes, I am still *all* of the above.

Involving alcohol in these situations also makes me a shit-talker. Thankfully, it's very rare that anyone ever calls me out on that shit-talking. Not sure I would survive those now in my golden ages. Although maybe all the childhood rage of a damaged soul would come flooding back.

Either way, alcohol has been my drug of choice to help silence the demons, or at least ease them somewhat.

Sometimes, it would seem the alcohol only brought out more demons or took me to an even darker hole. That's when I learned I couldn't (or shouldn't, because it was not the best idea to) drink when I was sad or down.

This realization actually brought me to a really good place in my life. If I was only drinking when I felt (mostly) happy about life, I would have an amazing time with friends—old and new. If I was feeling sad or down, I stayed inside my four walls: holding on, fighting my demons with all of my might, waiting for daylight to shine once again.

If the sun rose, so could I.

My journal keeps me company and helps me stay on task and on target. Which, ironically, allowed me to track my mood swings, habits, and especially the downers in my life. It forced me to choose the downers and allow that to continue taking me down this not-the-best-for-me path. Or to choose again, and this time, make it something happier or better than it was.

Obviously, the shedding began quickly. The shedding of the old skin that was no longer comfortable, no longer an accurate description of the woman I had become. The judgment of myself, the judgment from others about my lifestyle, my habits, my energy, my boldness, and my sexuality. They revealed themselves to be nothing more than another form of manipulation. Manipulation of the soul that I am, the soul that I want to be, and the soul that I am becoming. This path was no longer acceptable, as my soul now required more allowance, more acceptance of this soul to shine now.

Allowed, allowed without judgment. To just be me. Fully flirtatious and sexual at my young, beautiful, and amazing age.

My childhood had all of the makings of an exceptional gold-digging stripper, except . . . I wasn't. The force of balance came from my mother. Learn to do it yourself, and you will never need a man, never have to rely on a man, never look for a man to rescue you, and never have to wait on a man. Again, it would seem, my mother's control saved me from an even harder life.

The other side of that coin comes when, until I learned my own patterns, I found myself still challenging and competing with the men around me. Even the platonic ones. Seems completely irrational, but I was good at it, and it was my comfort zone. Until one day, one of these kind, gentle souls said to me that he knows I can do it myself, but that I shouldn't have to because he was here now and he could help make my life easier—the same way I made his life easier just by being here and being me. I also learned that by not allowing others to help me in this life, I not only take joy away from myself but also from them. The same joy I feel when I am able to help another human. Thankfully, I have now learned to accept and allow the help when it is offered. Even during those times when I *can* do it myself.

People often ask why I never had children. In fact, in most of society today, having children is some sort of status symbol. And, ironically, it's a trap for most men in those relationships. The rift in society today is that men are essentially "stuck" in these relationships even though women made the decision to keep or abort the baby, usually without any consultation of the male involved. No, usually, it was involving her girlfriends when the decision to keep or abort came up. Harsh. I know. But it's reality nonetheless.

The judgment of me not having biological children, the judgment of my sexuality, and my flirtatious behavior is all a falsehood. Accepting the truth of this manipulation has also allowed me to regain my freedom. My freedom as a woman, as a healer, as a worthy fucking human. My feelings are valid and accurate, even if others (or everyone) disagree. Even if the people I go to the most for guidance disagree with my behavior.

This is *the* tough pill to swallow. If your gauge of how you should live your life, how you should feel, what you should say, do, or think in this life says it's wrong, is it? Does it make *you* wrong? It has taken me fifty years to say, "Hell to the motherfucking NO!" It. Does. Not.

Society has taught us so many things, and not all of them are good. We are taught that sexual women are harlots, and therefore bad for society. This only points toward the responsibility being on the woman, not the man. No one ever asks why the man participated in the behavior. No one ever asks how that beautiful woman received that title. Or why we were taught to fear her rather than the man who supposedly loved us but did some mattress dancing with the local harlot.

Much like the witches who were burned, most of us were taught to fear the witches rather than the ones who burned them. Burned them, out of their own fears, their own manipulation of the truth. Burned them and taught the other women to fear them and thus pass that belief, that philosophy, on to their children, and their children's children.

Songs throughout the decades reflect and talk about women stealing another woman's man. Dolly Parton, Loretta Lynn, Patsy Cline, and even modern-day versions of the same shenanigans. I need to know if Dolly ever actually met Jolene. Did they have a conversation? Or was it all speculation, angst-filled, angry, and "crazy mind" behavior that led her to write this song?

Although, yet again, no one ever expects the man to own his part in the mattress dancing. Why is that? And why has it taken so long for someone to stand up and speak up about this?

Which brings me to this: if I have to be both the heroine and the hero in my own life, what the fuck do I need you for? I say this in silence to the man standing in front of me, simply asking me to dance. He has no idea of the crazytown standing in front of him. The poor guy just wanted to dance with a pretty girl. Angry much?

And, also, as I say this in my head to all the men who show up in my life that I feel are unworthy to be by my side but somehow worthy of a time or two between my legs. Unworthy because they will not survive me long-term. Unworthy because, the moment the vulnerable, soft Angel shows up, they will have no idea how to handle that extreme.

Why would I allow these men time between my legs if I already know they are somehow unworthy? Why are they worthy of any piece of me? Maybe Lyn missed the mark, and I am actually an honorary Scorpio male? Doubtful. But . . . if I had a dick, they would make movies about me, and society would congratulate me for it!

While I don't fuck anything that moves, I do find it disturbing that this behavior is condoned if you are male, but frowned upon (heavily, and even shunned) if you are a female.

Fuck those motherfuckers. Who is making these fucking rules, and how do we change them?

I want and deserve the ease of a relationship. The ease of music, of love, of laughter, the ease of sex and of intimacy. Surely, he is out there somewhere and feels the same void. A void that feels comfortable and also scary to allow anyone inside the forbidden walls that shield me. He is undoubtedly as fierce, vulnerable, and . . . as fucked up as me.

Clarity is about knowing who you are in any given situation. Sexually, in business, at home with your family, driving your car, or riding your motorcycle like a badass. Approval of anyone else, especially this historically patriarchal societal bullshit, is not necessary. Not necessary on any level.

My favorite friends have often reminded me that "my best" looks different on any given day. Still, give every day your best. When everything feels like *Groundhog Day*, and it doesn't seem to be changing, know that it *is* changing. The timing is perfect.

Take the shell off and be naked . . . or drown. Those are your options in this life. Own that shit and make your fucking choice! Life is just going to be big and messy, and that is how it is supposed to be. Life itself is a big, messy thing.

That's the definition of bravery, right? To keep handling your shit even when you are afraid. Even when you are scared.

Screaming through the self-denial and flagellation, I have now embarked on my own journey of acceptance, of healing, of unconditional love—for the badass woman I always was.

Powerful
Love

Enduring the level of trauma I did in my childhood, I had zero sense of self and zero self-esteem. With no idea who I was as a person, I became a "master masker." I was a chameleon of sorts, shifting, distorting myself to fit into whatever situation presented itself. *Smile and nod and glide, and smile and nod and glide.* As if I were in a constant beauty pageant that I was never going to win. I was a pretty little picture, keeping my mouth shut at least until I knew what I was dealing with.

The level of manipulation I learned from both of my parents, they learned from their parents. And as a recipient of this learning, I, too, was adept at telling people exactly what they wanted to hear and being exactly what they wanted to see. An unconscious training loosely grounded in love, damage, and trauma.

The truth, though, is that I was just a little girl who built a brick wall of shame, self-doubt, self-loathing, anger, and fear around herself. But she was lonely and sad, too. Peeking over and through the sturdy, thick layers of bricks, tree limbs, thick thorn-covered bushes and brambles, she knew she had to get out of there. A great big world awaited her, and surely she should be in it! Somehow, some way, someday, maybe.

What exactly are the rules of love, compassion, and kindness, anyway? As children, it would seem easy for us to learn those "rules." But what if no one ever taught your parents or grandparents? What if following your heart as a child caused you to get hurt, ridiculed, and abused? I believe we are all born with an innate sense of love, kindness, and compassion—for ourselves and each other. Our parents unconsciously teach us what they believe to be true about love, kindness, and compassion. Even when it goes against our very nature, we trust those around us to show us the "ways of this world." Our own survival is predicated on learning what we need to know to survive. We learn those things from those around us, especially our parents.

What happens when that child is taught that they are never safe? That they are unworthy, undeserving, and damaged? That they should never trust? The powerful love of our parents, no matter how flawed, feeds our distortion of reality. In general, I don't believe they meant any harm. They were simply teaching all that they knew, all that they had learned from generations past.

My love for my father led me to remove plug wires from my mother's car at his behest. My love for my mother and my desire to please and garner acceptance from her led me to step in and help take care of my siblings and her no matter what the cost to me—financial, emotional, mental, or physical—no matter what. Where do you go when there is nowhere left to go? This is the deep dive within, the shadow work about being damaged, causing damage, taking unnecessary risks, never feeling truly safe or fully loved. Acknowledging the level of trauma endured leads us to accept the truth of who we are.

What does it take for you to heal? Do you even want to heal? Can you heal?

Is it feeling of no value in this life, six blankets deep in an anxiety-filled river of tears, soaking the undeserved pillow under my self-flagellating brain as I struggle just to keep breathing? Hoping for the sun to come up so that I can pretend it is a new day, a new light, and possibly a new possibility for me?

Our habits and patterns, especially post-trauma, are hard-wired now. Any hint of trouble, and our mind begins playing those old tapes of survival, of heartbreak. We begin making life-altering decisions in the midst of this trauma mindset without realizing we have fallen into the pit. This is what psychologists call *self-sabotage*. And I—I am a master at this, too.

We wouldn't keep a friend around who was always putting us down, doubting us, or telling us we are not good enough. But what if that friend is yourself? The self-judgment is so much harsher and more consistent. Brutally consistent. And at the ready, any time a flicker of hope catches your eye.

Seeking approval, seeking validation from anywhere outside of ourselves is an absolute waste of our precious time and energy. In trauma environments, no one espouses this truth. It is up to the victim to seek direction in whatever form. A large number of us turn to religion, drugs, alcohol, or risky lifestyles, or we seek out abusive partners to perpetuate the pattern. Sometimes, perpetuation seems easier than dealing with the trauma. It's a sort of sick comfort zone, but I get it.

These days, with the internet widely available, there are all sorts of modalities presenting themselves to anyone willing to type it on their keyboard. We have to sort of feel our way through these options, too. All clunky and wobbly as we read through the possibilities, read the reviews, the well-meaning advice from others healing their own traumas. How do you know which will work best for you and your trauma? For me, it was a bold and audacious decision: try them all!

How do you know if you resonate with a particular religion or a particular philosophy of life until you've tried it? How do you know if your chakras are out of alignment or blocked unless you do some research on the matter? How can you trust the comfort, the relief in the words on the pages after what you've been through? Is that silver lining shimmering on the horizon real? Or is it another trick? A mirage, like those in the cartoons about the desert and the characters seeking water, only to find more sand, more trauma?

Those people from your past are warning you that you are headed down the wrong path. They say that can't be right—otherwise, someone else would have already tried it. Those who are new around you while you are seeking comfort, they don't know about your past, and fuck telling them now. It is too raw, too real, and too harsh. Just thinking about it makes the walls close in tighter, sucking all of the oxygen out of the room.

Besides, I need them to like me right now because they have information I want. Information about options to move this little girl out of the brick and brush.

As you might imagine, this little girl is stubborn. She never learned to be kind to herself. Only to others, and only in certain situations. She learned to be so kind as to apologize in the grocery aisle as she passed other shoppers. She wasn't even worthy to shop for groceries for herself. How could she possibly be worthy of a life worth living? She knows where she came from; she knows the secrets hidden away behind that sweet smile.

She knows.

It has taken me at least three decades of having the "way" repeated to me before I could accept it. Before I could accept myself. Before I could believe in myself, trust myself . . . or be myself.

So many signs, so many beautiful people, so many books, so many classes and lectures. I went through a constant seeking due to my disbelief and my distrust, especially of myself. *Surely,* I thought, *it isn't this easy. Surely, these people have never had any experience with the life I have already been through and must work steadily to keep buried deep, hidden, lest they know my secret and I am forever shunned, stoned at the prime of my life for trying to step out of my generational trauma.*

Surely, I knew my place in this world by now. And it was certainly not at the table with anyone who had any reason to be proud of themselves. No, that white, scalloped-edge tablecloth, fine-dining place setting including the dessert fork with a water glass and a wine glass, appetizer, salad, and an entree plate, just for good measure, a bread plate with its own knife, too— no, the likes of you have no business there, dear. Best move along before someone notices you.

Years of fits and starts. Years of writing, learning to meditate, learning about crystals, yoga, aromatherapy, herbal remedies, tinctures, tonics, sage, sweetgrass, palo santo, incense, and special candles. Supplements, sidecars, scotch, and gin. This is where it will begin. This is where *I* begin.

The repeating theme was *love.* With my trauma goggles firmly in place, I could not see this theme. I could not see the people doing their best to help me along the way.

Surely there was some fuckery afoot.

Time and time again, I tried to find someone to love, to show them that I was capable (worthy) of love, caring, and nurturing. Those behaviors have to be in there somewhere, right? And, surely, after they see how good I am at those things, they will love me back. After I take care of them and their every need, they will love me even more! Right?

Or they will take what they can get from me until I cry foul and push against my own precedence, stop showing them how good I am at loving them. But now I am proving that I am not really that way. Not really loving, kind, or caring. At least, that's what the tapes in my head would remind me each time another attempted relationship failed.

Some of my girlfriends would tell me I moved too fast in these attempted relationships. I knew I had to move fast before they saw the real me. Before they knew about my past and where I came from—who I really am.

That poor little abused girl from the podunk, generational trauma–filled, covered-up-with-a-field-of-cotton Mississippi. I knew they would run the moment they caught a good glimpse of her. So I kept her well-hidden. Even her "good" qualities. Yep, those needed to stay hidden, too. If you show them those, they will want to know more, thinking there will be more good stuff. But that's not how it is for me. The good is the icing. The cake is rancid—don't take too big of a bite, and don't get too close.

One of the gurus I listen to a lot says that a belief is just a thought you keep thinking. From the positive mindset point of view, I can grasp that concept. From the—it is still a lie even if everyone believes it—of it all, I struggle with that concept. The

"Fake it 'til you make it," notion still makes you a fake, at least some of the time. However, the mind is a powerful tool, and it is trainable. Over and over again, trainable. If you don't like your beliefs today, change them. Six months later, not digging that vibe . . . change it again. There are a few other gurus who say that what we believe, we perceive. This one didn't make too much sense to me until someone added that everything looks like a nail if you are a hammer. If I am expecting that everyone is there to cheat me out of something, cheat me out of my best life, then those are the people I attract to me, just with that belief.

There are a myriad of ways to reprogram our minds. Much like brushing your teeth, though, it is best done daily. One of the biggest reminders for me of how far I have come are my journals. When I feel as though I have not made any progress toward my goals in this life, toward being a better person in this life, I can read my journal from the past few months. Some days, it is only a line or two. Other days there are several pages of this life that I am thankful for. Pages filled with pieces that bring me joy, people that make me smile and laugh, thankful for my health, for my dear friends, a comfortable and cozy bed, a good vehicle, and especially my motorcycle.

Rereading through these helps me adjust my focus back to my goals, back to the many, many things with which I am blessed. The ability and the freedom to shift my focus during the dark days or the day after the dark day is probably what has kept me here on this Earth more than anything else.

Choosing to focus on the things I am thankful for allows me to appreciate just how far this little girl has come. How hard I have worked, the struggles, the people who stood by me during those times, and not giving up on myself. Each

Powerful Love

moment, we have a choice to make. Pursue gratitude and goals, or failure and regret.

In this past year, I have pursued gratitude and goals. When opportunities arose, I asked myself if I would regret not doing whatever the adventure was—talking to a new guy, taking the new job, writing this book. If I felt it would be something I would regret not doing, I did it. If it were something I felt I would regret if I did the thing, then I didn't do it. I simply walked away in the direction of my goals and gratitude.

Part of this walking away involved my thirty-year career. It had become burdensome—loathsome, even—to continue each day fighting to maintain a sense of purpose and direction. An opportunity presented itself to step away from this career, and I took it. There was an opportunity for me to make a "smooth" transition to the new company. At least, that's what their offer letter said. For me, it was a clear choice. It was so clear that I could not see any other path, no other options to stay in this rut.

This new company had some business dealings with some shady folks, including the one I was currently working for and already trying to leave.

I wanted no part in this. It came down to allowing my otherwise untarnished reputation to potentially be sullied if I continued on this path. I could not allow that to happen, even under the possibility of being unemployed and without income. This new company otherwise had a solid system and seemed to be headed in a good direction, sans the shady characters. It just wasn't good enough. I deserved better. Even if it meant being self-employed again and pursuing my own agency as I had done prior to my brother's death.

At the time, none of the options of staying in the industry felt like a positive. All of it was heavy, dark, exhausting, and unappealing to me. There was no fire left within me for this career path. It was time for a break. So I took a break.

This break allowed me to write this book. I am eternally thankful for that.

As I started the job, I had purchased a motorcycle. A little Honda Rebel 300 I call Bluebird. She has nearly 700 miles on her. Just as I was leaving the job, I bought a Harley Softail Street Bob. She has nearly 5,000 miles on her. The freedom when I am riding either of my bikes is indescribable. I don't have any fancy music options or cruise control, so it is just me, the wind, and her. Scanning the horizon for both danger and beauty. A perfect balance.

This new bike has a whole different feel, as anyone who knows bikes will attest. It was more than that, though. This new, faster, sleeker, sexier bike is more like the new me I am just now accepting. She allows me to lean into those curves more easily, tucking in, leaning, looking to the farthest "out" possible—chasing the mustard. You know, the stripes on the open road—one side is white like mayo, the other yellow, like mustard. I hate mayo, so I always chase the mustard.

She also afforded me some street cred with the Harley crowd. Especially when I rode her to Boise for the Ride for 22 without a windshield. Eighty miles an hour on a motorcycle, on the interstate, with Idaho wind? Not for the faint of heart. It borders on sadistic.

There's also the motorcycle family piece. It provides an opportunity to belong to a group that has your back, if for no other reason, than you ride. There are the hand signals between groups of riders that are pretty standard—for instance, if you see them patting the top of their helmets, there are cops nearby or within sight. There is also the sign we give each other when we pass each other. The "peace" sign but facing down. This is for two-wheels-down but also, it seems a signal of "I see you" as we roll past each other. This is especially true for me on the days when I am riding solo. It gives me a sense of peace within, like a welcome home sign at my favorite place.

Riding solo or with a group, out in the wide, open skies of the wild west fills me with such gratitude for life. There are those who assume if you ride a motorcycle you have some sort of death wish. This couldn't be further from the truth. At least for me, riding that motorcycle gives me a reason to stay alive—second only to my beautiful niece. My cobwebs clear out quickly and are replaced by the breathtaking scenery of Idaho, Montana, Utah, Wyoming . . . all of it. I find my soul filled with gratitude that I live in such a majestic place.

Peaking those hills as the world opens up to you, and the wind reminds you just how small you really are. Farmers and their families out taking care of the fields. Planes moving swiftly across the mountain bluebird skies. Wispy clouds and a hazy sun reminding you that you are indeed alive.

Fully alive.

Riding with my group of wind sisters adds an additional level of gratitude, connection, and family for me. When we are all out together, regardless of the size of our group that day, water ballet has nothing on the fluidity or function of this group. Leaving our meeting point, changing lanes, rolling through the countryside—it is an energy that brings life. Sometimes, I can hear that old song about "I move, you move, we move," when we each adhere to our responsibilities to ourselves and each other during our unchoreographed dance of the letting-life-go-for-a-moment ride.

For my brother's birthday this year, I did something different, too. Usually, I am closer to home, and my mother and I go out and put fresh flowers on his grave and have a chat with him. I was too far away this year. It occurred to me that because I could not save my brother doesn't mean I can't help save someone else's brother. Or sister, or mother, or father, or son, or daughter.

I rode with some other Harley riders to Boise, Idaho, for the Ride for 22. Ride for 22 is about Veteran Suicide Awareness. An average of twenty-two soldiers commit suicide *daily*. My brother's birthday fell on the exact day they were holding the rally this year. I considered it a sign from him for me to help someone else. I felt him riding alongside me during the four-hour ride. The tears I cried on that trip were the most healing tears I have ever cried in this lifetime. I could feel the release of the guilt, the release of the shame of my brother's death leaving my body. It wasn't mine, anyway.

I have always felt a draw to motorcycles. I was that kid who stood on the edge of the sidewalk as soon as I heard one about to go by and watched it until I couldn't see the speck anymore. Still do.

Some of the folks I ride with regularly ask me why I don't have music playing or some other kind of something in my headphones. For me, it is not about that. Riding my motorcycle is about clearing out the cobwebs.

Since that trip, I have also joined a group called Bikers Against Bullies. We ride to local schools and have an hour-long, fun-filled, role-playing demonstration with the kids about what a bully looks like. We also talk about how sometimes the bully is also hurting. How sometimes, the bully is being taught these behaviors at home. I know I was. Although I wasn't a bully to the little guy. I was a bully to the ones doing the bullying. If I saw a kid at school being picked on, I was the one who stepped in and mouthed off until the bully either swung or walked away. I had nothing to lose.

I also went camping. Sounds fun, right? I went by myself. I realized after I arrived at my campsite that I had never actually been camping by myself. There were always family or friends who joined me. The campsite was deep in the forest without cell service and no civilization for a good forty miles or so. That would have been a hell of a hike for help had something happened. It was an amazing experience that taught me more about myself than I expected to learn.

This journey has been a lot of self-care, self-love, self-compassion, self-nurturing. Lots of tears and lots of alcohol. A friend told me she overheard a lady at the wine store say, "My liver can handle what my heart cannot." I felt that. And I am thankful for this amazing body of mine and its ability to heal. The struggle to love the scared little girl inside, to encourage her to come out and play, to teach her/us/I we are self-sufficient, self-reliant, and worthy of an amazing life. In acknowledging my trauma, acknowledging the person I have become because of that trauma, and accepting that I can be whatever I want to be in this lifetime, has truly changed my life forever.

In taking the risks I have taken in the past twelve months—a motorcycle, camping solo, stepping away from my career, supporting causes that move my very soul—I have taught that little girl that she/we/I can handle anything this life throws at us. I can handle it with grace, with compassion, with love, and with pride, in the women we have become.

The most powerful love is me loving myself. Right here, right now, in this moment and every moment after.

It always was.

Never-Ending Tapestry

♥

As I was having dinner with some special friends, our conversation wound on and on, in random directions and back around. It made me fall in love with these people even more. This reminds me of how our lives are always never-ending quilts in our lifetimes. I say lifetimes because I am certain I have shared many with these beautiful women. It also reminded me of the afghan fiasco, as my grandmother tried to teach me the amazing art of quilting, crochet, and afghans.

In my late teens/early twenties, I spent time with my grandparents. Summers were harder because it was outside garden time in the Mississippi heat and humidity. Wintertime was much better. Winter allowed Grandma and me to stay inside and quilt or crochet the time away, listening to old gospel records. Yes, literally, old gospel albums on vinyl.

As I moved into my own space around age nineteen, I wanted to crochet a blanket for my bed. Grandma, a twenty plus–year veteran at crochet, advised me as to the length (the number of "hoops") I needed for a queen-sized spread. She reminded me, repeatedly, that as I went along, the yarn would stretch and not to get overzealous with my estimate. Did I listen? Um, *no*! I was a hard-headed, stubborn descendant of the most badass crochet guru in all the land. And let's be real. *How could she possibly know everything?*

Since I, of course, knew better, I didn't trust her calculations or expertise. I measured my loops alongside my bed for the "perfect" size. As it turned out, she knew exactly what she was talking about. Worse yet, it took me nearly a decade to crochet the "size" I felt was appropriate, and she never once scolded me for it. She did laugh a few times when I brought it to her to "check my work." Now, I know exactly why she laughed.

After all was said and done, this queen-size afghan turned out to be a king-sized duvet. Literally, I had to double it over and stitch it together because it was so big—and heavy. This adventure outlasted a number of relationships and bad decisions. It also taught me to at least consider the expertise of those who had already been down the road I have chosen. "The road" could be the tiny things, like how many hoops to start a queen-size adventure, or the road that leads us off the beaten path, to the goddess-size adventure that feeds our soul . . .

The never-ending tapestry or quilt of our lives and all of the people, pieces, and adventures that went into that creation is our own individual artistic expression to and of the world. This is how we see the world and how we *think* the world sees us. Or is that how they see us? That's a question we have to ask, especially those of us who have hidden behind our tapestry instead of expressing it openly. Where does that leave us? Do we have enough thread left to weave more? To weave a different and more beautiful extension onto our tapestry? I say YES! There is always more!

Each of us has our own threads of yarn, cotton, wool, nylon, silk, satin, synthetic, taut, firm, fat, thin, stretchy—all the threads. Our self-talk and our insecurities keep us bound up in our comfort zones, even though most of them really aren't that comfortable. Our own voice, our own freedom and joy, come from knowing we can weave our own addition to the tapestry of life. The tapestry of our life. The tapestry that makes us proud of ourselves and makes us want to share our beauty with the world.

How do we convince ourselves of our ability to simply weave a new piece of our life? Is it in our best interest to write down all the good stuff we see in ourselves during our good times, and then read those notes during our bad times? Or is it living in denial and pretending all is well in our world, allowing the wind to blow us in any which way?

Oddly, I feel it's a combination of all of those things. After all, this isn't a one-size-fits-all quilt. Know that you are stitching a new piece to your own tapestry with each new day.

Here I Am

♥

Throughout most of my life, if someone pushed me to that edge of do-or-die . . . I did it. And I never backed down. I went all in! No double-dog-dare or triple-dog-dare would stop me. Let's go! And, boy, once I stepped into the arena, it was on like Donkey Kong.

I am not afraid anymore. I am not ashamed anymore. It was not my fault.

I feel it is too late for me in a number of ways, but I also feel all of my life is now before me. A juxtaposition of choices made and choices that can be made now. Now that I am exposed for all to see, I would *like* to tell you that it feels amazing. As if I were running naked down the street, screaming like a banshee, with the tears of my newfound freedom streaming down my no-makeup, no-filter face with my head held high, shoulders squared.

That isn't anything close to the truth, though.

It feels more like standing still with my arms splayed open, my head hanging down, watching the tears fall straight to the floor. Tears that never wash the soiled truth from my skin on their way down, eventually buckling under the weight of my own fears, my own self-administered beatdown filled with all of the doubts and insecurities I've carried for the past five decades.

Each of us moves through our lives in whatever way we are taught, whatever way we believe to be the best direction, the best action for us. Courage is being who you are through the fear, shame, and self-doubt. Through the potential ridicule and public shaming. I have never been that brave or courageous until now.

Choosing this journey was not an easy choice, nor has it been an easy road to travel. I never expected much of what has transpired during this journey. We all expect a few tears and maybe some tiredness and a desire for extra sleep or extra alone time. Ha, a few tears! There were *lots* of tears, and many, many boxes of tissues. There were a lot of long periods of sleep and rest followed by more sleep and more rest. I'm thankful I had that luxury. In choosing this journey and stepping into it fully, there were also physical manifestations I did not anticipate. My face broke out as if I were a teenager again. My digestion was back and forth, from bloated to starving to not hungry at all, and nothing tasted good, anyway. My shoulders ached with the release of the long-held tension of expectation, disappointments, and wondering what was going to happen next.

My tolerance for noise became an obstacle as I desired quiet to write, and my environment was not conducive to quiet. Worse, it was out of my control to achieve the quiet. Alternatives such as headphones or breathing through the noise to reach the silence inside are how I got there, how I got *here*. My heart is pounding out of my chest writing some of these words. Red hot, fire-filled tears were burning my cheeks as they fell into my lap. Long were the nights I spent crying myself to sleep, forgiving myself for carrying this burden alone and with so much shame. I had extensive, deep conversations with myself, spilling the honest truth of who I am, how I felt then, and how I feel now. I did this without self-judgment— only with compassion and forgiveness could I tell my truth to myself now. Hot showers allowed the water to spill over me like a waterfall, washing away the tears, washing away the sins, washing away the hurt. Hot baths soothed the physical aches that came with the releasing of my truth. For days my eyes were swollen and burning from the tears of the night before, and I was unable to wear my contacts.

Sometimes I wanted to escape so badly I would go hang out with strangers in a bar somewhere. Just to escape my own head. My own heart. The smoke alarms went off from all the sage and sweetgrass I burned each day.

I am thankful that I made this choice and also thankful for the lessons I have learned along the way. I have found a new kind of strength within myself and an appreciation for the woman I have become. I acknowledge and appreciate all that I have been through, all of the calculated risks, the adventures toward who and what I want to be in this life. I hold a deep gratitude for the woman I have become, knowing my inner little girl is safe now. Now, now we can grow together.

Friends and strangers alike who hear only portions of my life tend to have the same reaction. Usually it's something along the lines of: "You're so brave, I could never do something like that," or "You are a total badass. Holy shit!" None of those things registered with me as a reality until I began writing this book. The moving cross-country or driving coast-to-coast solo or learning to ride a motorcycle at fifty years old—these things all seemed like a natural progression of my life as I knew it. As in, there were no other paths that felt right for me in those moments, so, of course that's the path I chose. This book, and exposing the truth, my truth, is also one of those paths. I could see no other way.

Exposing this truth now doesn't help those who had come before me and not those who came before this book avoid their trauma. But maybe exposing this truth will allow others to heal. And maybe it will help others be saved from this trauma in the first place. At least, that is my hope.

As I meditate now, I can see the Valkyrie within me. She is covered in scars—some healed, some still in the process of healing—sword in hand, slaying the false beliefs of my past, the fears, the betrayals, the abandonment of myself, and also by others. All sliced open, pulsing onto the hard ground beneath my feet, spilling their lies onto Mother Earth where they will be transformed into mulch for better use as fertilizer. A fitting end to the lying pieces of shit they are.

As she stands there, chest heaving with each weighted breath, sweat, blood, and tears flooding down her body, releasing the toxicity, releasing the falsehoods of long ago, boldly and courageously she takes one step toward her future. It is just one step. It is the step of a new beginning.

A new life.

The culmination of all that I have been through, all that I have seen, felt, tasted, and touched in this life, are weaving together now. And I can see them much more clearly. They are weaving the tapestry of my life. While it is far from completion, I can see its pure beauty now—its flawed perfection that is my life.

Epilogue

Speeding through this trajectory of my life on an uncertain, unstable, and borderline incendiary path, there seemed little choice or option for anything other than the road I was on. There's an old quote that says, "Why do you always choose the hard road?" The response is, "Why do you assume I see two roads?"

I feel I am not alone on this hard, lonely road. The footprints of those who have gone before me are still fresh in the Mississippi mud and clay. Some are beginning to harden in the scorching heat of the formidable sun. Where are they now? Did they survive their own demons? How did they get out? Were they given another option at the last possible moment that changed their lives forever?

From the moment we are brought into this world, our soul knows how this is going to go, and it may not look like what we have in mind as young adults: wading through the trauma, struggling to survive and not drown, and sometimes attempting to save others along the way. Scratch that—it definitely won't look like what we had in mind. Sometimes we forget that others are their own people with their own needs, feelings, and perceptions. The closest version of unconditional love we can reach for is to trust our own instincts, make peace with ourselves, all while allowing others to make their own way. The only thing that will save us from ourselves is to fight back the demons in our minds, our hearts, our souls. We must know we are not alone while we charge courageously into this battle, giving us strength to endure the long nights meant to destroy us. In the end, the most powerful love is the love you show yourself because it shines and spreads to everything and everyone around you. Show up, show out—be your own badass self.

There are those who will say that we are fully healed when we can tell our story without crying, without an outward expression of emotion. It is my fear that we forget about those emotions. It brings me to tears to read my story each time and think about those who might have been saved had I been braver sooner, had I been more courageous sooner. It is my fear that we push those tears and those emotions so deep down that we forget they exist. That we forget we are human.

I never want to forget. Our emotions and the release that come with crying those hot, sobbing tears is a reminder we are human but also a reminder that others have gone through the same or similar circumstances. If we can't feel those emotions anymore, our empathy for another human being's journey is altered. Then where does that leave us? Empathy for one another and ourselves is part of the healing process.

There are other humans like us who suffer in this world today. All day, every day. It is our job as humans to shine our light for them to find a path to lightness, a path that may not be their own but could lead them to their own. Society will try to make you feel ashamed of being brave. As if to say, *If you can survive all of this, why are you complaining? You are doing all right.*

Fuck them. I am doing all right because I had no other choice, motherfuckers!

The very fact that I am surviving—nay, thriving—in your fucked-up world is proof positive I am a badass motherfucker. That does not mean, on any given day, that you might find me crumpled on the floor in a ball of rage and fire-filled tears. Shortly thereafter, though, I will rise like the phoenix and hold my ground with the best of them.

Every day, we will live to fight another day. Until we don't.

This . . . this is my beautifully flawed and also perfect life.

Acknowledgments

This book directly interprets my life from my perspective, emotions, and jaded vision based on my view of the world at that time. Putting all of this onto paper has not been easy or quick, and with the band-aid still clinging to my skin, I needed help taking those final steps. I thank those who helped me traverse this path, navigate my healing, and move forward to a life worth living.

My go-to friends for balance, guidance, talk-me-off-the-ledge-without-judgment with their varying degrees of toughness for whom I will be eternally grateful—in this life and all the ones after—Makalani, Cinimon, Janeene, and Tune.

For giving her all, and all her best efforts to rein in this wild freedom-seeker, my mother, Patricia.

For the best and most compelling reason to still be on this Earthly plane, my Scooba Snack.

For encouraging me to live life now, rather than waiting, and for tempering my hot-headedness over and over, many, many thanks, Mr. M.

For building my courage and showing unconditional love to me as one of your own, I thank Ms. Jackie.

For chasing the wind with me, keeping me grounded and focused on becoming the best version of myself: my Idaho family, Kim, Maureen, Penny, Laure De, and all of the Idaho Falls Litas.

For all of the open talks about food, religion, family, work, money, crocheting, and quilting, rest in peace, Grandma Mae.

Last, and mostly, I am thankful for my writing coach, lady Meredith. She believed in me when I couldn't believe in myself, encouraged me, and guided me to the path of completing *Flawed Perfection*.